Becoming a Grandmother

Becoming a Grandmother

A Life Transition

Sheila Kitzinger

SIMON & SCHUSTER
A VIACOM COMPANY

Simon & Schuster Ltd
West Garden Place
Kendal Street
London W2 2AQ

Simon & Schuster of Australia Pty Ltd
Sydney

A CIP catalogue record for this book is available
from the British Library

ISBN 0-684-19619-0

Typeset in Caxton Book 11/13pt by
Palimpsest Book Production Limited, Polmont, Stirlingshire
Printed and bound in Great Britain by
The Bath Press, Bath

Picture acknowledgements

Page vii   © Rob Judges, 1989. First published in the *Daily Telegraph* (Ewan MacNaughton Associates)
Page 1   © Judy Harrison (Format Partners)
Page 11   Picture Bank Photo Library Ltd
Page 23   © Nik Wheeler (Art Directors Photo Library)
Page 47   © Zephyr Pictures (Art Directors Photo Library)
Page 59   © Earl Young (Art Directors Photo Library)
Page 73   Art Directors Photo Library
Page 87   © Marc Grimberg (The Image Bank)
Page 103   © Uwe Kitzinger
Page 125   © Steve Niedorf (The Image Bank)
Page 143   © Lupe Cunha
Page 159   © Walter Hodges (Art Directors Photo Library)
Page 185   © R. Chapple (Telegraph Colour Library)

Contents

Ourselves as
Grandmothers

This book is about an important transition in the lives of many women, of which little has been written and which is often not even acknowledged as a life transition: becoming a grandmother. It is about how we see ourselves as grandmothers, our often complicated and ambivalent feelings, and about our relationships with our adult children and their partners – how they see us and how we see them – and with our grandchildren. We are expected to take being turned into a grandmother, whenever and however it happens, in our stride, and to make the switch from mother to grandmother smoothly and effortlessly. But for many of us it is not quite as simple as that. Even when we get pleasure from being grandmothers, we want to be able to reflect on what we are doing and to learn how to do it well.

In my studies as a social anthropologist of birth and in my work as a childbirth educator and counsellor I explored the experience of becoming parents. As I did so I learned a lot about families, and often about grandmothers, too, not only in Western societies but in cultures all over the world. When I became a grandmother myself, I realized that nothing had been published except, on the one hand, very serious sociological and psychological academic papers and books and, on the other, light-hearted, jokey books intended to jolly grandmothers along.

So when I started this research I decided to ask for help from grandmothers and mothers through magazines and newspapers in the United States of America, Britain and Australia. More than a thousand women replied and told me about their experiences. They answered a detailed questionnaire, which included many open-ended questions, and sent often lengthy letters, some of which I was able to follow up with interviews or further correspondence. I made opportunities for group discussions with women and their daughters and daughters-in-law in places where I was lecturing in the Far East, North America, and Eastern and Western European countries, too, and I have included what I have learned from these women.

When I became a grandmother I had no clear idea of how I wanted to be or what my daughter expected of me. I certainly could not have put it into words. I just hoped it would come naturally. So I faced a major life transition without any understanding of what it entailed, what the challenges might be, or what my daughter wanted. I suppose that I had a negative picture consisting of what I did *not* want to become – interfering, know-it-all, bossy or sentimental, for example – and neither my husband nor I saw ourselves as what Stephen Spender called in one of his poems 'cardboard cut-outs of grandparents', eagerly waiting for the grandchildren to visit but peripheral and largely irrelevant to their lives, while the real action took place elsewhere. I wanted to go on being *me* and not have to fit a stereotype. My identity did not depend on my being a grandmother. I did not need, nor even particularly want, my daughters to have babies. Perhaps that was partly because I had done the 'baby thing' in a big way, having five children – three under two, four under five, and five under seven – and had committed myself to motherhood with gusto, and gone on from there to write about birth, do research and have daily involvement with mothers and babies. My life felt richly satisfying and I was certainly unlikely to romanticize grandmotherhood. I accepted that my daughters had their own lives to live. Some were lesbian feminists and did not plan to have children, and I was happy with that.

Tess, who made me a grandmother, fell in love with a fellow student at university, married and went to work as an electronic engineer in the United States. Six years later when I visited her there she quietly announced, 'I'm pregnant.' It was all very low-key. So low-key that I asked her whether she wanted the baby. She did. I remarked that she did not seem to be bubbling with excitement. She said, 'I didn't think you'd approve.' That was a shock. She explained that I was so approving of her academic sisters and those who were carving their careers that when she chose marriage and motherhood she feared that I might think it was second best, a waste of her potential. I remember feeling rather ashamed about that.

In fact, each of my daughters is unique. I do not want to impose a pattern, even if that were possible, of giving good marks for achievement only to the ones who write theses and give lectures. But clearly my enthusiasm for writing and research must have made Tess feel that I might be disappointed. The truth was that I was thrilled that this was something – the bearing of a child, becoming a mother, with all its joys and problems, that had been an important life passage for me – and one that I could now share with her.

My daughter moved back to England toward the end of her pregnancy and she and her husband came to live with us. The birth of Sam took place in a birthing pool in a sunny garden room just outside my study. I cradled Tess's head as she floated in the warm water, two lovely midwives watched and waited, and she held on to her husband, Jon, as contractions mounted like great swelling waves and the birth energy swept through her. The months after were an opportunity to discover the warmth, wisdom, and sheer common sense of my daughter as a mother and gave me the pleasure of watching a new life unfold.

In many ways I am writing as much about daughters as about grandmothers, because I am exploring the territory in which the relationships between mothers and daughters and daughters-in-law take place after the birth of their children. Daughters make all sorts of assumptions about how their mothers will respond to being told that they are pregnant, about how they will feel about their grandchildren's behaviour, the way their daughters run their homes and manage (or fail to manage) their children, and the dynamics of family life. The same goes for daughters-in-law and mothers-in-law. When we become aware of their expectations, hopes and fears, it is worth stopping to think, 'Why does she expect that reaction of me? What is she telling me about my attitudes not only about what I have said and done, but also the unspoken messages that I have sent her?' In my case I think my daughter's doubts about my reaction to her pregnancy pointed to the struggle that I had experienced as the wife of an Oxford don and a mother of five to make space for myself and to be able to achieve anything apart from motherhood. I used to write in the early mornings before the children were awake. There were many times when a child came into the room to be told, 'Wait a moment. Let me finish this sentence.' (Since we live as an extended family, this is a situation with which my grandchildren are becoming familiar too.) When I went on my first anthropological field trip to Jamaica I took with me all five children as well as a young woman to be a helping hand. I would go up into the hills to interview women at six in the morning so that I could get back home at three in the afternoon to be with the children. I had to organize my time meticulously and I am sure that Tess had noticed how exhausted I sometimes was by the evening and yet determined to juggle family and career. She saw the price I paid, and is wary of that kind of over-commitment.

We communicate to our children the things that matter most to us, often without even knowing that we are doing so. It is not only a matter of struggling to build a career while at the same time being a home maker and mother, or of pouring out energy into helping people outside the family as well as within it, from personal moral commitment – which is how it was for me because I wanted my children to grow up ready in their turn to challenge social injustice, inequality and the abuse of power. We may also be saying that everything must be clean and tidy in the house, that children should always be polite and well-behaved, that we must be careful not to neglect the man of the house, that we should not let our children impose on us but get out and about and enjoy ourselves, or we may put particular stress on religion or politics, on keeping up with the neighbours, or on our grandchildren's academic achievements, social skills or excelling at sports.

For me, having grandchildren is a bonus. My identity is not encased within the grandmother model. I can approach the tasks and challenges lightly and enjoy being a grandmother in a way that I see some women cannot, often because they are anxious and trying hard to make everyone happy and show that they are in control, or because of their need for personal gratification and to know that they are loved and the centre of attention.

As I explore family relationships in the pages that follow I hope to reveal some of the hidden messages conveyed between mothers and daughters and mothers-in-law and daughters-in-law and the reactions and responses that they stimulate. I am writing also about the way we perceive ourselves as grandmothers today, how we saw our own grandmothers, and the contrasts between those different images. I explore our feelings and values, the demands that are made on us, and the stresses and satisfactions of being a grandmother. I describe how we behave in tricky situations and find ways of resolving conflict; and focus, too, on all that we can learn from the grandmother experience.

In this book I am deliberately not writing about men. Although women describe how they see their partners as grandfathers and their sons as fathers, it is not my purpose to tell about the lives of fathers and grandfathers. That research still needs to be done. The spotlight here is on *women*.

While I discovered women who were exuberant in their role as grandmother, it also emerged that many others were troubled. Marginalized within the family and disempowered by the wider society, some felt burdened with all the problems and felt none of the joys of being a grandmother. I aim to reflect as honestly as I can the challenges that women confront as well as the pleasures they experience.

I believe that some readers may meet in these pages women who are very much like themselves. They will see how other women cope, perhaps realize that they are not alone with the problems and challenges they face, will be helped to enjoy themselves more as grandmothers, and may grow a little wiser. For becoming a grandmother can reveal new aspects of the self, bring opportunities to learn and develop as a person, to build a network of rich and satisfying relationships, and to see the world with freshness and vitality through the eyes of a child.

Turning into a
Grandmother

M any women are surprised when they become grand-mothers. They had not expected it to happen just then or in that way and even if they longed for their child, or child's partner to get pregnant, the reality can be quite a shock. One reason is that you are nudged, whether you want it or not, into a different generation, and the simple act of someone else getting pregnant changes your view of yourself and alters your relationships with those close to you.

Being turned into a grandmother – a choice you did not make yourself in any active way – propels you into territory as yet unmapped. You are on marginal land, picking your way over ground which lies between motherhood and being a respected 'tribal elder'. Just as on your first day at school, when you had your first period, when you had sex for the first time, or committed yourself to another human being, when you were pregnant, and after the birth of the baby, becoming a grandmother constitutes a life passage. It is an important transition in your life.

When a woman is expecting a baby there are books, maga-zines, classes – all useful ways of preparing herself for the challenge ahead, and of getting the vitally needed information that replaces fear with knowledge and enables her to be aware of options and alternatives. When she becomes a grandmother there is nothing like this. She may feel in limbo.

Though there are classes to prepare for birth, grandmothers are left to cope on their own. Occasionally you come across newsletters with titles like *Creative Grandparenting* containing articles describing how 'Hugging can improve your health', and there are the textbooks used in adult education classes on 'Achieving grandparent potential'. But in general grand-mothers have to pick up ideas about how they should be, what they ought to do, and what it is considered normal to feel, by sheer chance from other women who have been through the same astonishing, bewildering transition from mother to grandmother. A woman with a year-old grandson writes, 'I had no idea what to expect at any stage in the process of having grandchildren . . . We were in unexplored territory, tentative in each step and anxious to make no mistakes.'[1] The transition to being a grandmother can be as difficult as the transition to motherhood. The grandmother role is superimposed on that of mother, too. Being a grandmother involves complex and intricate relationships in which you are both mother and grandmother, and if your own mother is alive, a child too. As the writer Rachel Billington puts it, 'The most important point about a mother, your mother, is that she is your mother for always. Your one and only mother. Your mother for all time. You cannot divorce your mother.' You go on being a mother to your adult children until you die.

For many women becoming a grandmother is something more. It is a symbol of ageing, of being 'past it', no longer at the centre of life, just a spectator on the touch-lines, the invisible older woman. You are someone's mother – someone's grandmother – but, you protest, also you! However happy a woman is at the news of the coming baby, it is often a greater milestone in her life than the menopause. Some women say that they get a hint of their own death – and suddenly time seems awfully short!

There is a much more positive aspect of this awareness. The baby represents the continuity of life and the future after you are gone. In a strange way, with the birth of a grandchild you are yourself reborn. When it is a daughter who gives birth, as you watch her mothering you remember and relive your own mothering of her. Perhaps this is one reason why grandmothers often say that they feel much closer to the children of a daughter than to those of a son.

You may be deeply involved in the lives of your grandchildren – even, sometimes, taking the place of a missing mother. It may be great fun. For many women there is an intense shock of pleasure in having this little new person in their life, which comes as a total surprise. A woman whose marriage had just broken up, who had to sell the house, and whose son was leaving to live abroad, but whose daughter had just had a baby, said, 'It's the one bright thing in my life! And it's wonderful!' But for some women it is very different. After the initial pleasure they come to see being a grandmother as a trap. They may feel put upon, with the parents taking it for granted that they are available for child care – when they have their own lives to live. Other grandmothers are cut off from grandchildren by distance or problems with relationships in the family, which result in them being isolated and alone.

Being a grandmother can bring emotions of joy and intense pain: pleasure in being able to share the new life emerging, a personality developing and growing strong, loving and being loved, and pain from misunderstandings and family conflicts, when parents split up, if there is violence or sexual abuse, when children get into trouble, or when there is illness or a child dies.

When adult children turn to you in need, and after them their children – even perhaps their children's children – you realize that mothering never ends. You may have thought you were taking on something for twenty years or so at most. Now you realize that it is for life. If there is family breakdown or if lives crack under the strain, you may feel it is a re-enacting of a tragedy. Can we never learn? It is easy to slide from there into feeling personally responsible for all the problems in your children's and their children's lives.

Many women are not sure what to do when the going gets tough. They cannot model themselves on *their* grandmothers or mothers because times have changed and the whole situation is completely different. They have been sucked into a role that they do not know how to fill.

In a study of the life cycle of American women as wives, housewives and mothers, published in the early seventies, Helena Lopata asked them to rank a woman's different roles in the family in order of importance. Whereas 45 per cent thought that the combined roles of wife and mother were important, only 3 per cent attached any importance to the grandmother role.[2] I suspect that an even lower percentage of women today think grandmothering is an important part of their lives – until, that is, they suddenly find that they are grandmothers and are not at all sure of the part they should play.

Seeing your child with her own child brings a sense of wholeness and completion. But there may be disturbing emotions, too. From the vantage point of experience, perhaps you see a daughter making the same mistakes that you made, are aware of the same tensions in the mother–child bond as those you

experienced years ago. There are the same quandaries and
confusion, the same hope, the same despair. You may long to
warn, to counsel, but you know you must stand back. On the
other hand, becoming a grandmother may make you far more
critical of how you were as a mother. 'My daughter is doing a
better job than I did,' one woman says. 'I wish she had been
my mother.'

If you think back to how it was when you first became a
mother, you may remember times when you had momentary
glimpses of how it felt to be mothered when you were a baby.
That often comes as a great surprise. As a new mother touches
her child she recollects how it was to touch and be touched.
There are tactile memories of the feel of skin on skin, firm
hands cradling, a little body being soaked in the bath and,
floating in water, how it was to look up into her mother's
smiling face, to be lifted – damp, hot and hungry – from a cot,
being bounced on a knee, patted on the back as she hiccuped
and felt bubbles gurgling inside her, and the excitement of
raspberries blown on her tummy. Memories like these help her
empathize with her baby. But there may be painful elements in
this, too – memories of being handled roughly or impatiently,
being gripped too tightly or pinched, memories of being in
the hands of people who touched in ways different from her
mother's touch and, for some women, flashes of memory of
sexual abuse. Similar memories are kindled in grandmothers,
too, and they are often vivid and totally unexpected.

When a woman turns into a grandmother she not only
remembers how it was to be a mother, but also how it was
to be mothered when she was a baby herself. There are layers
of meaning, strata of experience, which add depth and colour
to her observations of her daughter or daughter-in-law with
the baby – how she touches and the baby responds, how they
look into each other's faces and find each other the two most
fascinating people in the world – and she may recall keenly
and instantaneously, and sometimes with a sense of loss, the
charmed circle created by that mother–baby bond.

A grandmother who witnesses the strength of the tie with the
baby sometimes feels left out, deprived. This may be because
she herself never experienced such depth of love, or cannot
remember it however hard she tries. If her own babyhood
was emotionally impoverished she may be painfully aware

of what she has missed. And if, as a mother, she held back from giving herself completely to her baby, because experts advised her not to pick up the baby when he cried, not to comfort him by rocking and cuddling, never to take the baby into her bed, and not to offer her breast whenever the baby nuzzled for it, she may now be painfully aware of the bondage of regulations which shackled her as a mother, and which prevented spontaneous, loving behaviour. She grieves her loss. She may long for her daughter or daughter-in-law not to make the same mistakes or suffer the same restrictions that she did. Or she may feel jealous, and express her envy in criticism of the younger woman. In one grandmother's words, 'Everything in that house revolves around the baby. He's lovely, but if she gives in to him all the time like this he'll never learn self-control.' She is anxious that her daughter's mothering style is very different from how her own was forced to be. It is hard for a woman who disciplined herself to fit a model of motherhood which restricted her with a tight corset of rules and left her feeling discontented and cheated, to allow herself to enjoy a daughter whose mothering style is relaxed, warm and spontaneous.

When you become a grandmother you reflect on the ways in which *you* were mothered, too. A woman in her forties had 'twelve blissful years bringing up four children'. But her own mother, a teacher, who married just before the Second World War, and enjoyed using her qualifications during the war, was sent straight home when the men returned afterwards, and hated the constraints of being a mother stuck in the house with small children. 'I was born in 1947, and had to endure the anger of a frustrated teacher, who, although she loved us, hated every moment of domesticity.' She goes on to say, 'I can't convey the relief we felt when she returned to work once my sister started school, and for us normal childhood began.'[3]

A grandmother may be frightened of the freedom the younger woman appears to have, anxious that the baby will be harmed, that the daughter will be made captive by a baby whose every wish is satisfied, or that the couple's relationship will suffer – and, perhaps, her son be neglected – because the baby has become the sole focus of a daughter or daughter-in-law's existence.

A good deal is written about a father's possible jealousy of

the baby who has taken the woman he loves away from him
– but nothing about grandmothers' feelings as they remember
their intense experiences as mothers, experiences that hurt and
sometimes produced great suffering, as well as those that were
warm and satisfying. Yet over and over again as each woman
becomes a grandmother and every baby is born, she relives
her own past, her personal, intimate, secret experiences both
as a mother and as a baby herself. She may even relive intense
feelings of when her mother had another baby and fear that
she will be shut out from her daughter's love, replaced by a
baby once again. A psychoanalyst who was having disturbing
dreams during her daughter's pregnancy commented, 'I'm
afraid I'll "lose" my daughter after the birth of the child, as
I "lost" my mother when my brother was born . . . Mother,
father, sister, grandparents, all very much neglected me for
the new prince . . . Now I'm terrified of a repeat performance,
that I'll lose my place in Janet's family as I did in my own, that
I'll lose my wonderful daughter, perhaps my dearest friend.'
She thinks about the other set of grandparents. Perhaps Janet
and her husband will turn more towards them and neglect
her. 'Will I have to compete with them for my grandchild's
affections? Generous, kind and loving, also rich, they will be
some competition . . . It's hard to believe I won't be crowded
out again.'[4]

Knowing how to be a grandmother does not come instinc-
tively, any more than knowing how to be a mother simply
flows in a woman's blood. Nature may help, but basically it
is a learned activity. We do not know how to fill this often
difficult role just because we are older and have managed to
struggle on through the years. Wisdom is not an automatic
gift of age. Many older people bristle with prejudices and
assumptions, cherishing rigid attitudes which hinder thinking
and the freedom of ideas. The years may bring a narrowing
of vision. Some older people exist in a self-centred and ever
diminishing world of small personal satisfactions and irrita-
tions, whether it is concerned with having a house clean and
tidy, shopping, food, coffee mornings or bridge, or the annual
holiday in the sun.

The love we have for our grandchildren, our concern about
the life that lies ahead of them and the kind of world that they
are going to live in, is a stimulus for us to actively reach out to

make that world a better place. For age brings wisdom only if we learn, and go on learning.

In these pages I hope to give you an opportunity to prepare for being a grandmother, and to cope better if you are one already. Being a grandmother propels you, whether you like it or not, on an exciting journey into the future. It can give insight and understanding, and bring the deep joy of giving and receiving love.

Images of the
Grandmother

The baby lies in her cot wearing a pink dress, and everyone says how pretty she is. The happy bride smiles for the photographer, orange blossom in her hair, a spray of lilies on her arm, and a white satin dress flowing to her ankles. Wearing a frothy pink négligé, her blonde hair streaming, the new mother sits in a rocking chair with her baby cradled in her arms. Then the silver-haired grandmother, carefully coiffed, is being advised and reassured by her insurance agent, bank manager or doctor, hearing his news with gratitude and relief. She sits in the twilight as she knits, looking fondly at her grandchildren playing at her knee. Or she walks hand in hand with her distinguished looking white-haired husband on the sea-shore or in a flowery meadow, both in the sunset of their lives and bathed in a rosy glow. She is carefully preserved in spite of heart trouble, arthritis and failing short-term memory. She is a grandmother. Or here she is a Third World woman, her face etched with a thousand wrinkles, like cracked mud in an eroded river bed, all the suffering of her tribe in her deeply set eyes, her hands reaching out to beg a crust of bread, a bowl of rice, her starving grandchildren around her. An altogether coarser image is that portrayed by the *Daily Express* cartoonist Giles, whose nightmare character of Grandma, with her black garb, padlocked handbag, felt hat and menacing umbrella, was a threatening stereotype of the ageing woman as the witch of an industrial culture with its mean streets of chip shops and day trips to Blackpool pier.

These are the archetypes of woman from cradle to grave, recurring symbols appearing again and again in newspaper stories, cartoon strips, advertisements and on TV. They are the crude moulds into which women are pressed, symbols in the code for being female.

The medicalization of menopause

Many women first become grandmothers around the time when they are experiencing the menopause. We often already feel under threat for this reason alone, in a society which puts great value on female youthfulness, and where increasingly doctors are warning women of the potential dangers of not having hormone replacement therapy. Right through life women are treated as victims of their raging hormones – suffering from a disturbed endocrine system which makes them irrational, angry, anxious – and often mad. We are seen as vulnerable to physical and mental illness when we menstruate and – above all – when we cease to menstruate. From that point on, the uterus is perceived as not only redundant but also treacherous. In the seventies the standard American obstetric textbook, *Williams Obstetrics*, stated authoritatively, 'The only known potential of the uterus, other than to house products of conception, is to harbor disease.'[1]

In the past, middle-aged women who went to the doctor were likely to be treated as hypochondriacs. They were a nuisance and doctors thought they were imagining their symptoms. Today the menopausal woman is the object of much concerned medical attention, 'a prime target for the new prevention-orientated general practice', as Sandra Coney puts it in *The Menopause Industry: a guide to medicine's 'discovery' of the mid-life woman*. 'Research careers are being built around her, and there are doctors and medical entrepreneurs who wish to measure her bones, her breasts, the cells on her cervix and her hormone levels. People build machines that can scan, photograph, X-ray, and magnify the most intimate parts of her body. The pharmaceutical companies have a veritable chocolate box of pills, patches, pessaries and implants for the mid-life woman. She can swallow them, have them sewn into her flesh, or even insert them in her vagina – from where the magic hormones will course through her body transforming everything they touch.'[2]

Normal, healthy women become grandmothers at the same time in their lives that they are treated as potentially at risk of crumbling bones, sagging uteruses, and collapsed vaginal walls and bladder supports. Life after the menopause is perceived as a degenerative state in which a woman's uterus and vagina atrophy, she loses her femininity and vitality, and is prone to depression and other psychiatric illnesses, and hormone replacement therapy is promoted as the elixir of youth.[3] All this, and being turned into a grandmother too!

Has-beens

Traditionally, grandmothers have always lived with or close by their daughters or daughters-in-law and their families, and have often controlled a large female workforce based on the home. They have always had a hand in raising children. They have been needed to rock the baby's cradle, to sing lullabies, to soothe a crying baby, as another lap to give security and comfort, another strong body to cool and clean, and – as children grew – to teach the skills of the culture. They have told stories about how naughty their grandchildren's mother or father were when they were little, building bridges between present and past, between a child's life and the lives of parents and grandparents, and fashioning a web of family myths. Their grandchildren have learned from them fables, legends, chants and hymns, and watched them enact religious ceremonies that communicate the core values of the culture. The Balinese grandmother arranges fruit and flowers on the altar and presents them to the gods with a prayer, and even the two year old copies her actions. They have had an important role in economics, in teaching and in the politics of the community. The very word 'grandmother' is a mark of respect. The Japanese *oba-san*, for example, is a member of a venerable group, and after years of subservience to men emerges onto 'the glorious plateau of independence and freedom' from the restrictions that younger women must endure.[4]

In many traditional cultures the grandmother is the key person in helping a child through all the transitional rites of birth and infancy. If she is not around some other older women must represent her. Without her the child cannot develop. In Northern Australia, the Aboriginal grandmother is needed for the smoking ceremony which is considered important to keep a baby healthy. She it is who rocks the baby through the purifying smoke of the fire of konkerry branches and leaves sprinkled with her daughter's breastmilk, which links the child with the ancestors from 'creation time' and protects him from all harm. In cultures all over the world it is the grandmother's hand that guides the young child, her brain that stores the memories of her people, her mouth that speaks with the voice of the ancestors, and her loving arms that protect a child from bad magic and from catastrophe.

In Western societies, in contrast, grandmothers are above all ex-mothers, women who have finished doing a task. They may be allowed to have a hand in mothering, and to re-enact mothering spasmodically and in a modified way with their grandchildren when they baby-sit and at family get-togethers, but they 'play' at mothering, and this only on occasions when it is agreed to by the real mother, or in a crisis when their help is sought because she is unable to cope or is absent.

When a woman gives birth to her first baby she symbolically replaces her own mother, who is then supposed to retire into being a grandmother. Some tender nostalgia about her own previous experience of mothering is tolerated, but she is now on the sidelines.

Whenever the media run a story about a woman who happens to be a grandmother much play is made with it. She is a pathetic, vulnerable victim, an amazing achiever in spite of being elderly, or she has criminal propensities. The picture drawn by a TV critic writing about a documentary on the great white shark is typical of the repulsion and disgust that the image of the grandmother conjures for men: 'Doesn't that gummy mug remind you of a grandmother napping shark-jawed without her dentures?'[5] A recent haul of headlines in the British national press reveals 'Daredevil Granny does a freefall parachute jump', 'Supergran jumps for joy', 'Grandmother robbed at knifepoint', 'Grannies dumped at Christmas' (a story about hospitals deluged with elderly patients when families are on holiday), 'Grandmother of eight gets degree', 'Sweet granny masterminds world's largest counterfeiting ring', 'Horror house grandmother speaks after multiple murders', 'Trim and trendy grandmother models clothes', 'Golf-cart grannies' (who live it up in Palm Beach, collecting their dividends and their welfare money, too), 'Grandmother hooked on heroin', 'Gun-toting granny – the fastest gun in Britain', 'Housefire kills grandmother of ten', 'TV sex – but not in front of our gran' and a feature entitled 'What shall we do with granny?' Men who are grandfathers are never presented in this way. They exist in their own right.

The author Margaret Yorke, who writes suspense novels with themes of rape, mutilation and murder, says; 'People are always shocked that a grandmother should be writing novels like mine. I find that attitude terribly patronising. I just tell them I wasn't born a grandmother. No one would ask Dick Francis what a nice grandad like him was doing writing all that indecent stuff!'[6]

The basic stereotype is that grandmothers are homebodies. We are frail. We like our food. We have to be humoured and indulged, or we will invent excuses to avoid baby-sitting. A granny decorative tea-cloth sums it up, 'Always treat your granny like a greenhouse plant, kept warm in the sun and with plenty to drink. Give her lots of photographs for her albums and photo-frames. Invite her to stay and furnish her with bedsocks, a night cap and hot water bottle and in the morning a cup of tea or breakfast in bed with flowers on the tray. When she comes to babysit have a nice warm fire and provide a box of her favourite chocolates. Then she'll read best-loved stories to the children and darn their socks when they've gone to bed. Let her enjoy spoiling her grandchildren with sweets and toys and never complain about lipsticky kisses. If she's old, help her by running errands and finding her spectacles and knitting. Always compliment your granny on her cooking and often ask her to make your favourite food. Above all make her feel needed.' The saccharine folk wisdom on this tea-cloth, like that represented on cards for granny's birthday, implies that if you hate sewing, can't cook, never get round to putting photographs in albums, don't gorge yourself on chocolates, wouldn't be seen dead in bedsocks, and don't readily succumb to flattery – and if you find your grandchildren interesting personalities but are nowhere near being besotted by them – you will never make it as a grandmother.

Stories written for children and school readers reinforce such images of the grandmother in the same way that they reinforce rigid gender stereotypes, with grandpa fishing and grandma cooking, grandpa reading the newspaper by the fire while grandma knits. In a French children's book Grandmère is a frail little silver-haired woman who wears steel-rimmed glasses and spends most of her time in the kitchen making and serving food for her grandchildren and their friends. They call her 'Grandmère Chocolat'. She constructs marzipan baskets filled with edible flowers and houses out of spiced bread, chocolate and nougat. When she is not cooking she knits or washes the dishes. One day a child visits and finds her house empty. She has fallen and broken her leg. In hospital she lies in bed worrying about the children. They make her a gingerbread house and take it to her with messages on flags stuck on the roof, 'Grandmère, I need a pullover', 'Grandmère, you haven't finished the story about the fox', and so on. This brings immediate recovery. She gets up, goes home, cuts the cake for them to eat, and contentedly continues her life of utter devotion to her grandchildren.

Children themselves often cling to such stereotypes. When they draw pictures of their grandmothers – even ones who go on African safaris or run their own businesses, who are lawyers or professors, or who have taken up rock climbing or parasailing, they usually base them firmly in the home, engaged in gentle tasks like gardening or cooking, and doing things for *them*. A grandmother who has shoulder-length black hair, and who is teaching her eight-year-old granddaughter to play tennis, was startled to read her school essay about 'My Grandmother' in which she described her as a white-haired old lady who walked with a stick. Such images give a comforting security.

Perhaps that is what it is all about – security. Children usually experience their mothers – even the most laid-back mothers – as powerful authority figures. The love they feel for their mother is 'ambivalent, contaminated with anger at being disciplined, jealousy of siblings and rage at the necessary disappointment and frustrations of growing up', says a psychoanalyst who is herself a grandmother. She believes that the 'love of a grandparent is less polluted'.[7] Grandmothers can be moulded into an image which is more easily controlled and far less threatening, especially if they are transformed into frail, dependent old ladies.

Challenging stereotypes

Women are now challenging the stereotypes and protesting against the restrictions of the gender mould. Many do this as they come to crisis points in their lives, when they are forced to look at themselves and ask who they really are and what they want to be; with the birth of a baby, on being made redundant, at the menopause, or when a loved person dies, for example. For some women it is not until they become grandmothers that the enormity of these crude stereotypes hits them or – even if they were aware of them before – that they pluck up courage to challenge them in their personal lives.

As I talk to grandmothers, I realize that to find yourself suddenly assigned a new role and be expected to play a different part in the drama of family life, is an opportunity to examine your beliefs. It can also be a politicizing experience.

In the past most grandmothers probably slipped easily into their roles. Because becoming a grandmother concerned their domestic life and personal relations and family, they were unlikely to identify the transition as having anything to do with politics. Passing on intimate secrets and advice to daughters, sharing and recording their pleasures, their doubts and worries – about a daughter's pregnancy, a child's health, a baby's pretty ways and first achievements – these things form the substance of many journal entries and letters between mothers and daughters. The emotions women felt as grandmothers, the problems faced, did not, for the most part, lead to analysis or overview of how other women, in their own and different societies, experienced this transition. This is still often the case today. For 'women's distinctive experience as women occurs within that sphere that has been socially lived as the personal – private, emotional, interiorized, particular, individuated, intimate . . .'[8]

Women have always struggled to cope with difficulties in their lives as if they were a consequence of some inadequacy within *themselves*. We thought we were not good enough mothers; we did not love our husbands enough; we were not sufficiently intelligent to manage maths or science. It was our fault if we became pregnant by accident or could not hold on to a pregnancy, and when we were sexually harassed or raped we believed that we must have sent out the wrong signals, and were responsible for what happened. We blamed *ourselves* and apologized for our own suffering.

Think of how we react to the stresses of housework, our feelings about being overweight or having an eating disorder, about contraception, abortion and infertility, how so often we blame ourselves if we get depressed, and the sense of guilt we bear when we fail to care as well as we want to for the young and the very old and all those who seek nurture from us. We can only begin to understand our experiences as women in a context wider than that of our personal lives.

How grandmothers used to be

It may be hard for us to imagine that our grandmothers ever fell in love, were sexually aroused, and had the passionate, tender, overwhelming emotions that *we* experience. It takes an enormous effort of imagination to think of how they might have been before they were encased in the grandmother role. This may be partly because in the past women aspired to be grandmothers. It was – and still is for some – the culmination and reward of motherhood, a major achievement in a life's journey. They settled into the role with satisfaction; they knew the appropriate behaviour and could enjoy a new status in the family; they could warn their granddaughters about the intentions of young men, the risks of sex, the hardship of women's lives; they could advise them on how to feed a husband, how to patch up quarrels and how to rear their children. In large families grandmothers *reigned*. A woman remembers that all her grandmother's seven children, their partners, and the fifteen grandchildren went to visit every single Sunday 'to pay homage as if she were royalty' and 29 people crowded into one room in a small terrace house.[9]

Go back fifty years or so and these grandmothers knew who they were, and would recognize each other. They might be sorrowing widows dressed in black. They were often figures of stern authority. Sometimes they were cantankerous trouble-makers who spent much of their time criticizing younger members of the family and the husbands or wives whom their children had married. They were the keepers of family history and tellers of tales of long ago. Often too, they felt the respon-sibility of upholding family morality and, from their imperious matriarchal position, were lawmakers in the domestic group. Many were strict disciplinarians in a way that is no longer possible, and when the young sloped off and did their own thing they mumbled and complained. They had front parlours with lace curtains and delicate china cups, flower-decorated and gilded. They wore buttoned shoes which were done up with button hooks and, in winter, rubber galoshes that squelched in the rain. They smelled of violets, eau de cologne, patchouli and cachou, and they knitted, embroidered or did intricate crochet or tatting. In cold northern towns they were the glimpsed faces, framed by curtains, keeping an eye on the neighbours and whatever the young were getting up to. In warmer countries they sat on rocking chairs on the front porch, watching the world go by, and in Mediterranean villages were hunched figures under black shawls sitting outside their doors from sunrise to sunset, while the old men played *boules*. At the well or the communal laundry they assembled in groups, cackling like old hens, sharing the gossip, pronouncing verdicts on the young. At café tables in sophisticated cities such as Vienna or Paris they sipped coffee, each with a lace ribbon round her throat, wearing flowered and feathered hats, and at soirées and balls they would scrutinize the activities of the young through their pince-nez. And those who were poor worked as women have always done – till they dropped – hands, knees, feet, swollen and gnarled like twisted branches of vine, spitting blood and mucus, eyes clouded with cataracts, hearing gone. There was little effective treatment for the diseases of age. To become old meant pain born with fortitude or constant complaints – often too, crippling illness and a wandering mind. People aged earlier then. Though we shall probably live longer, we shall never be as elderly as our own grandmothers were.

This is one reason why many women are astonished and bewildered when they become grandmothers, and protest, 'Oh no, I'm not ready! Not yet!' They remember their own grandmothers; they see their mothers as grandmothers and they feel they are nothing like them, and never could be. They could never have the authority, or the narrow-mindedness and prejudice, or, perhaps, the sweetness and selflessness. They could never be still and contemplative, or be so sure of themselves. And they could never give up on life, watch other people being active, while they were content to dwell on memories.

As one grandmother told me, 'I didn't feel old enough. I thought grandmothers were grey (I colour my hair) and plump, wore aprons, knit and sat in rocking chairs. This wasn't me, so I couldn't believe I was going to be a grandmother.'

It is not surprising that we do not recognize ourselves in the figure of the grandmother we knew in the past. We need to create a positive role model for today's grandmothers. We are not crusties, wrinklies or crumblies. We are not old bags, crones or hags. We are *ourselves*!

How Grandmothers really are

Grandmothers are, of course, never just grandmothers. They have multiple roles, though their grandchildren think of them exclusively as 'granny' and their children think of them largely as mothers and grandmothers. When talking to grandmothers it is clear that many vigorously resist being seen in this one-dimensional way. As a result, there is tension between what is expected of them as grannies and their other interests and commitments. It hurts when these are trivialized or ignored, especially when a grandmother feels under pressure to become an invisible older woman who is valued only in so far as she is of use as baby-sitter and gift-giver.

The public image of grandmothers has not caught up with how grandmothers of today really are. Middle-aged and older women are usually not sitting around grieving the loss of their children, feeling lonely, wondering how to fill their empty days, and pathetically grateful for any chance to baby-sit or see the grandchildren. It often comes as quite a surprise to older women themselves that their lives are so full and satisfying. Those who expect that when their children leave home and have their own families they may suffer the 'empty-nest' syndrome often discover a new freedom.

A study of working-class women in London in their forties, fifties and sixties revealed that close on half experienced higher self-esteem, less helplessness, more social confidence and believed that they were more intelligent and more in control of their lives in these years than ever before. Thirty-five per cent thought they *looked* better too. As a result they were happier than when they were younger, and by the time they reached their sixties they were especially unlikely to be depressed. In their forties and fifties perhaps, but in their sixties they were blooming! They said that their children were much easier to get on with as adults than adolescents and that as they had grown older other relationships had improved too. Many were promoted at work, had started up their own businesses or gone into higher education.[1]

Once past child-bearing women often have fresh energy. They are determined to make the most of the rest of their lives, and are busier than ever before with things they *want* to do, not things they have to because children need to be clean and fed. 'I feel that parts of my life are just starting,' one woman told me. 'So don't grandmother me to death please.' A grandmother who works in a community theatre, plays the accordion in two bands, started to unicycle in her fortieth year and juggles, is now learning to paint and to write. Myrtle Allen is a renowned chef who runs an Irish country house hotel with her husband, six children, their partners and some of her twenty grandchildren, an example of how a woman can enjoy her family and be a great achiever into the bargain.

Children often describe their grandmothers with admiration for their vigour and the antics they get up to, 'My Gran can cycle faster than any granny in our street. She can do the most groovy dances I've ever seen. When she does her exercises with Jane Fonda she can do them much faster than me and never has to stop', 'She's trendy and likes pop music', 'She makes funny jokes' and 'Her hair is ginger and she is absolutely crazy'.[2]

Grandmothers with zest

Becoming a grandmother is more often a middle-age than an old-age event.[3] For many women today this is a time when, free of immediate family responsibilities, they discover new skills and are at last able to do what they really want to. And the idea of old age is also changing. Women in their sixties and seventies do not get old. Instead we enter an active and satisfying 'third age', and after that, at eighty, a happy and contented 'fourth age'.

The market in magazines for older women is developing, and organizations like AARP (American Association of Retired Persons) in the United States of America are springing up. AARP's motto is 'Bringing lifetimes of experience and leadership to serve all generations' and it has more than 32 million members aged 50 and over. It was started back in 1958 to better the lives of older Americans through service, advocacy, education and volunteer efforts. Members give their time and talents in community service, further education, health care and quality of life issues – with emphasis on women and minorities, on workers' rights and retirement planning, and on exploring the future roles of older Americans in society.

Projects of this kind flourish because of a dramatic change in the social landscape. One fifth of the population of the United Kingdom is now over 60. It is estimated that by the year 2000, 35 million Americans will be 65 or older, and in Japan, which has the world's longest life expectancy, by 2020 one in four citizens will be over 65. In the early years of the twentieth century, when old age pensions were first introduced, only 5 per cent of the population of Europe was eligible, the rest had died. Now a quarter of the population of Europe is already of pensionable age and there is an increase in the proportion of families who have living grandparents, and in the total number of grandparents. A survey in the mid-seventies revealed that approximately three-quarters of Americans over sixty-five have grandchildren. Nearly half of them see them every day, and three-quarters see them at least once a week.[4] But whatever their age, and even though they see their grandchildren regularly, grandmothers are often so busy that baby-sitting and getting down to the chores of regular, practical help for their children and grandchildren is either intermittent or out of the question.

The French author of a book for grandmothers writes that a grandmother's tasks should be to keep the family united, offer help when it is asked for, spread the latest news, recall the past, and provide for the whole family a place of refuge.[5] It sounds lovely, but however much you want to offer all these things, it may prove impossible to juggle your other commitments so that you can fill that fairy godmother role. There has been much discussion in the media about working mothers who have to juggle their lives, about the resulting stresses on them and their children, and the plight of 'latchkey kids'. It should be acknowledged that for many grandmothers life is a complicated juggling act, too, and that whatever they do they are left feeling guilty.

There is a common idealized image of how grandmothers were in the past – always on hand and delighted to have the children round. But, though geographical distance or a woman's commitment to her career often rules out any consistent grandmother care today, in the past, too, grandmothers were often not available to baby-mind. In medieval times many women did not live beyond their twenties, and mothers had often died when their children had their families.

In the United States during the Depression extended family support networks were broken down by poverty. The 1930 White House Conference on Children described the situation, 'First the payments on the home began to be stopped, and then the home went, and the furniture went, and then the credit was exhausted at the grocery store, and then the family moved in with another family, and they shared as they could, and circumstances were such as to produce nothing at all to share.'[6] The result was that, though mothers much preferred grandmother care, children often had to be handed over to social agencies who placed them in foster homes. Families were fragmented and relatives often lost all contact with each other.

Once the Depression was over many working mothers once again relied on grandmothers. A Gallup poll of 1943 revealed that 46 per cent of mothers did not want to send their young children to day nurseries and preferred child care to be given by someone in the family or by a close friend.[7] But as the war continued the grandmothers went to work in war factories or took over jobs that men had vacated to join the armed forces. Patterns of grandmother care, even in Afro-American families where they had been well-established, broke down again as women worked in factories, tanneries and on the land. Either the father worked a day shift in the factory, while the mother worked both the factory night shift and a day shift looking after the children, or the children had to be placed in foster care, surrendered to institutions, or simply left uncared for.[8] The grandmother who is not around to help and who is busy with her own life is therefore not a new social phenomenon.

Very few grandmothers turn out to be elderly ladies who wear lace and use lavender water. Many are still – at least potentially – in their own child bearing years. A woman in her forties may have a baby in a second marriage at the same time as her older child from a previous relationship gives birth or may have babies who become aunts and uncles younger than their nieces and nephews. If her daughter delays child bearing until she is in her thirties, a grandmother may have young children who will be aunts and uncles when they are still only three or four years old themselves.

You can also be a grandmother even when you have never had children. Perhaps you have had years of infertility, repeated miscarriages, or have lost a child through stillbirth or death in infancy. Women with no biological children of their own acquire instant families when they enter a relationship with someone who already has children and grandchildren. At 39 Sheri is step-grandmother to her husband's grandchildren. She has an infertility problem and can never have children, but finds great joy in these grandchildren. If a woman has longed for a child but been unable to have one, this can herald a deeply satisfying and unexpected stage of life.

On the other hand, if you have never had children it may be hard to realize just how chaotic and demanding life with them can be. You may have a romantic, unrealistic idea of how families are. It is the same when a grandmother has forgotten or pushed into the background of memory the stresses, storms and tempests of everyday life with young children, and fails to recognize just how shattered a mother feels when she has somehow managed to get through the day but is left feeling completely used up and utterly consumed by her family by evening. The further away you are from the realities of raising children, the less likely you are to understand how demanding it is, and the temptation may be to put your needs first.

In any family there are bound to be individuals who jostle to be in the limelight. When you are a grandmother rivalries are played out on a wide stage. There are demands for your concentrated attention, and insistence on everyone having equal shares of your time and love. Family dramas like this often involve large casts, with children, their partners, their partners' parents, siblings and partners' siblings, your partner, and your parents and parents' parents. Direct comparison is made between the beliefs, attitudes and behaviour of each set of grandparents as parents and as grandparents, and of sisters and sisters-in-law, brother and brothers-in-law as mothers and fathers, and the behaviour of their children. Secrets are shared – and passed on – hints dropped, rumours spread. You may discover that you are at the hub of anxiety, intrigue and conflict.

Seeing yourself with fresh eyes

Though you may have expected to feel older when you became a grandmother, there is a good chance that you will feel younger and develop a new image of yourself. When you become absorbed in children's play, tell stories, sing, act the clown, laugh with them, you may discover all sorts of things you had forgotten you knew how to do. You are relaxed, tolerant, creative, imaginative – even frivolous. One woman told me, 'I thought I'd be a strict old bag, but I have surprised myself. I'm really quite wonderful! And I look younger every day.' The odd thing is that with this expenditure of energy you gain *more* energy. Filling your time with activity, you *find* time to do things that otherwise you could never have fitted into your busy days.

You also rediscover yourself as a child, for playing with children gives you an opportunity to relive your own childhood. When a one year old examines a daisy for the first time, you see it with new eyes too. When a three year old first ventures into the sea and feels the rush and pull of waves, you experience this excitement anew. When a child tastes ice cream for the first time, it is like the very first ice cream that startled your own taste-buds. A woman who has stiffened up a bit and usually sits on chairs, gets down on the floor to build a castle, runs to catch a toddler, plays piggyback and ring-a-ring-a-roses. She enjoys singing and acting nursery rhymes. She is stimulated in both mind and body.

You can rediscover the pleasure of play – doing things for sheer fun. One woman says of her grandchild, 'He has brought such joy into my life, such fun and laughter.' She has learned to play before her work is finished and her grandchild is 'a perfect excuse to blow bubbles, play clay, crayon, and build forts.' Another comments that for the first time she is able to go to places and do things that you can only do if you have a child to take with you, 'It is a chance to capture my childhood again.'

Being a grandmother brings the satisfaction of giving and receiving love, sometimes more freely and more generously than ever before. A Mexican colloquial term for this is to 'chipilear' one's grandchildren. It means hugging, touching and pleasing them. A Mexican grandmother says, 'I see they do their homework, I feed them, I "chipilear" them. They know I wait for them with emotion.'9 'I've two more people to love,' says a granny of a six and a two year old, 'and they love back without reservation.' She believes that this affection is more difficult with your own children. 'Parenting is complicated by the need to discipline and set standards. But as a granny, I follow rules the parents have established, and within those boundaries I am free to love those kids to excess. I have never had any other relationship so completely free of emotional complications. As a parent I felt I had a job to fulfil with my kids; as a grandparent my only task is to love them.' This grandmother is surprised at the keenness of the love she feels, 'When I leave them after a visit I feel a physical loss. I never before understood the cliché of "feeling empty", but that describes my physical sensations. When I say goodbye to my daughter I am sad, and I certainly miss her, but it doesn't have the same impact on me.' Other women discover that the love they feel for their grandchildren deepens that which they already have for their children. One grandmother describes how this is part of a 'new fabric of love for and from my children. The grandchildren give to all of us a new form of energy. I feel I am growing with all of them. Being a grandmother has enriched my emotional life, as well as my relationships with my children.' This sense of growing and developing as a person is a common and often unexpected part of the experience.

Being a fully involved grandmother keeps you young. It can stimulate thinking, force you to be physically active – you don't need a personal exercise trainer when you have grandchildren, and if you hold in your arms a new-born baby and lovingly identify with your daughter as she suckles her at the breast it can infuse your circulatory system with oxytocin, the hormone of love.

If you only meet your grandchildren occasionally you may miss out on all this. But if you are the baby soother, the toddler cuddler, the playmate, the one who clears up chaos after the room has been turned into a jungle or a dinosaur swamp, the story-teller, the one who runs holding onto the back of the bike when your grandchild learns to cycle, the person who tries to find answers to a constant 'why?', the one who invents fresh occupations every ten minutes for a child who is ill in bed, who helps a child discover the pleasure of reading, kneading bread dough, digging new potatoes, going for long walks to find wild blackberries or the remains of a Roman camp, you have to put off old age till another time.

When a grandchild is born all relationships in the family shift and change. A woman often discovers that she becomes closer to her daughter, and many mother–daughter conflicts begin to be healed once the younger woman is herself a mother. The same can happen with a daughter-in-law. You meet on common ground – your love for the child. You also meet as women in a new way now that you are both mothers. You may find that you enter a new relationship with your son, too. You see him in a different light as a father and watch as he matures in his relationship with his child and his partner. Grandmothers often describe with delight how their sons have changed, dropped their macho image, and become caring and fully committed fathers, revealing a tenderness of which their mothers had not been aware before.

When your partner turns into a grandfather you see new aspects of his personality, too. He may be as much involved as you are with the grandchildren, or he may pull back and be uncertain about his role.

Grandfathers

Enthusiastic grandmothering is not necessarily matched by equally enthusiastic grandfathering. The degree to which a man becomes involved in being a grandfather is often a replay of how he was as a father. Many men were tied up with their careers when their own children were small. Grandmothers say that they usually take responsibility for grandchildren, that their male partners are willing to help, but rarely initiate, and that they only begin to give priority to doing things with the children as they develop interests which they can share.

Whereas women often see their grandmothering as being in a very different style from their mothering, and are sensitive to changes in child-rearing practices, grandfathers often stick to the established system and the old rules, and are bewildered and on the defensive when told that things have changed. As one woman says, 'He is unable to get close to them. He is still haunted by old ideas of how children should "behave".'

A grandfather usually, as one grandmother put it, 'sets more limits on his time' and 'can switch off when he has had enough of them'. 'He really loves her,' another says, 'But I have to encourage him to get involved playing with her.' She comments that this is how he was with his own children. It seems that many grandfathers have an amused, emotionally detached and slightly wary attitude to their grandchildren, rather as if a group of marmosets were let loose in the house.

Grandmothers often adapt gracefully to having toys all over the floor, crumbs thick on the table and even in the bed, drinks spilled on the carpet, and happy chaos everywhere. (I admit that this is one of the side-effects of being a grandmother that I find difficult.) But grandfathers may not be so tolerant. They are often bothered by children's noise and mess. One woman says of her husband, 'He is completely at a loss when things get out of hand.' Another, whose husband is 'a perfectionist', says, 'He hates it when the little ones wander around with ice cream or chocolate biscuits leaving sticky marks on the furniture and palm prints on the windows.' It did not sound as if he was the kind of man to have a damp cloth handy and be willing to clear up himself, so this made an extra burden for her, and she had to act as a buffer between the children and their grandfather, and stay cheerful and apparently relaxed whatever happened. Grandfathers are sometimes resentful that care and attention is directed away from themselves and onto the children. The result is that when grandchildren are around many grandmothers face extra work not only in caring for them, but also in looking after their partners and making sure that they do not become too stressed.

On the other hand, some men become far more involved in the care of grandchildren than they ever were with their children. 'He's much better than he was with our own children,' one grandmother says, and another says that her husband idolizes the grandchildren and has a 'simpler' and easier

relationship with them than she has. Many men missed out
on time with their own children because they were working
hard outside the home. But, once retired, they have more time
and can relax, join in a child's games, and listen. An engineer,
for example, spends hours with his grandchildren 'making a
skateboard ramp or bird-boxes', although he is 'not a "natural"
with small children'. A step-grandfather is 'marvellous. He's
easy-going but firm, and much loved by the grandchildren'.
Another grandfather has a specially close relationship with a
seven-year-old grandson who suffers from cerebral palsy, 'He
is kind, patient and loving, and they share a love of basketball
and Celtics.' Peter first met his grandson when he was three
months old, and formed a close bond with him. They did not
meet again for another eight months and both grandparents
were prepared for being treated as frightening strangers. But
not a bit of it! Their daughter walked off the plane 'and as
soon as Elijah saw Peter he held out his arms to him, and
hardly let go the entire three week visit.' Now that he is
older, the little boy mimics his grandfather's mannerisms
and constantly proclaims, 'Grandpa is my best friend.' The
adoration is mutual.

One woman says she is taking delight in seeing her father
recapture his sense of fun and enjoy his grandchild, and
suggests that men may be more willing to cast aside their
inhibitions than women. If that is so perhaps it it is because
women usually bear the responsibility; while a grandfather
plays with a child a grandmother is probably thinking about
what she must cook for the next meal and whether the laundry
has finished its spin dry cycle.

Many men feel they must work with their eyes on the future
and find it hard to enjoy the present. Then, when they retire,
children have left home and it is too late to create intimacy in
family relationships. As a result, they have closer emotional
contact with grandchildren than with their own children.

Women sometimes say that their partners are better with
teenagers than little ones, although other men, who were close
to the children when they were little, draw away as they turn
into teenagers and bring an alien culture into the home. Teenagers are exposed to risks and to challenging situations – hard
drugs and HIV infection, for example – which are outside many
grandparents' experiences. When a grandfather's advice is not

taken he may try a heavy-handed approach or react by avoiding contact with a young person with whom it seems impossible to build any bridge of communication. A grandmother, on the other hand, often goes on nurturing and caring.

Fractured families

Grandmothers have often been through broken marriages and started out on a new relationship when their children are producing babies. This is reflected in greeting cards on the market, 'To Mum and her husband' and 'Dad and his wife'. They are preoccupied with an experience which demands their time and energy. It is hard to juggle the needs of children and grandchildren with those of a partner who may either not appreciate the claims made on you because he has never had children, or who has lost contact with his own children. If he already has a family they may also have to be fitted into the crowded timetable of visits, birthdays, holidays, baby-sitting, shopping expeditions, family meals and outings.

In Britain today, for every two marriages there is one divorce.[10] Grandmothers may get caught up in the animosity and suffering integral to an adversarial divorce system and as a result lose contact with their grandchildren. Noreen Tingle, who works with the Grandparents' Federation, says that grandparents who are denied access to their grandchildren sometimes stand outside the school looking through the railings just to catch a glimpse of a loved grandchild. 'One grandmother heard that her grandchild was going on a school trip, so she stood on the docks at Dover for five hours in the hope of seeing her – she didn't, but the hope kept her going.[11]

It is painful for children, too, when they are not allowed to see grandparents whom they love, or when grandparents reject them because they are angry and side with a divorced son or daughter against the other partner. This is what happened to the journalist Julie Myerson, who was six years old when her parents' divorce went through. 'At the height of his bitterness about our parents' divorce proceedings, Daddy decided not to see us any more. Granny never contacted us again either. The last time I saw her, I cycled four miles to take her a bunch of buttercups picked in the hedgerows. "Thanks for the weeds," she'd said.' Julie goes on to say: 'Granny Pike lived to be a very old lady. When she died in a nursing home – barely visited by her son – she hadn't seen us for eight or nine years. But we later heard she'd had photos of us by her bed – pictures of three little girls, frozen in time. It was a dark snowy day and we were nearly grown up when a nurse rang from the home. "Mrs Pike has died," she told us. "She thought you'd want to know." It was typical of Granny to make contact, finally, just as there was no more contact to be had.'[12]

If children come to live with them after their parents' marriage breaks up, grandparents are virtually plunged into parenthood again. For a woman who was a full-time district nurse, and whose son returned to live with his parents, bringing his two children, aged five years and 13 months, this was very stressful. She said, 'I'm glad I'm here to be a parent, but I'd like to be just their nana. It made me cry when I had to be the disciplinarian. I envied the two hours they had with their other grandparents because they could devote time to them – with us it was cook, clean, wash, feed, go to work. I felt the girls got more out of those two hours than in a week with us.'[13] Far from grieving over her empty nest, a grandmother in this situation is forced into trying to manage a very overcrowded one.

Divorce and remarriage means that many grandmothers are enmeshed in a wide network of blended families: children, step-children, grandchildren, step-grandchildren, and their partners and relations. When a relationship breaks up and a couple remarry, grandparents often have to share their grandchildren with step-grandparents who are virtual strangers.

One effect of broken relationships is that there is often no one to tell the story of the family and maintain a sense of its own history. Grandparents have a new and important function in a culture in which serial marriages are increasingly common. They ensure continuity for children, a quarter of whom have experienced the divorce of their parents by the time they are sixteen.[14] As one woman put it, 'I am their fixed point in a changing world.' A wise grandmother welcomes new partners into the family, while also listening to and respecting the confidences of grandchildren, helping them come to terms with their feelings of loss.

When grandparents themselves have divorced, the arrival

of a grandchild may bring a new and satisfying link between a man and woman who could not stand living together, but can enjoy being grandparents together. The involvement of other members of an ex-spouse's family – great-grandparents, aunts and uncles – may draw families together even when the grandparents themselves are hardly on speaking terms. Helen's ex-husband has moved thousands of miles away, but his family live in the same area as their daughter and grandchild and they now form a close family network. She has fallen out of love with him, but loves his parents and brothers and sisters. Relationships often have to be worked at with delicacy and tact. One woman asked her step-grandchildren to call her by her first name because she did not want to compete with her husband's former wife as a grandmother, and since then they have become good friends.

A daughter may start a relationship with a man who already has children and then have her own baby. A woman whose daughter married a man with four children admits, 'I am longing to spoil my daughter's baby, but she wants me to treat all the children the same. I do care about the others, but it is difficult to make a pension stretch to cover five Christmas presents.'[15]

It is often claimed that extended families have vanished. Far from it! This is a new form of extended family. It can be developed in a very positive way when relationships are good. As one seven year old says, 'I am lucky, luckier than most. Most people have two or four grandparents but I have six. Six kisses, six hugs, six smiling faces . . .'[16] In blended families, as in traditional societies, grandmothers are at the hub of multiple relationships. Although in many parts of the industrial West, especially in urban areas, the traditional extended family with members living in the same household or in close proximity to each other has all but disappeared, you may be coping with a new form of extended family which is even more complicated and demanding.

Mothers and daughters: losing intimacy

Now that places all over the world are pulled closer, distances covered greater, the speed of travel increased, we whisk from one country to another half across the globe in the time that it would have taken our great-grandparents to get to the next city in their own country. Electronic communication links people's thoughts and makes possible rapid negotiation, business deals, the almost instant realization of multinational schemes. Yet people often feel lonelier, more cut off, than ever before. Global communication cannot replace community. Multiple interlocking networks cannot make up for the loss of intimate personal relationships.

Mothers at home with young children, and elderly people who no longer have meaningful relationships in the family and workplace are those most likely to be isolated. In spite of phone, fax and camcorder, regardless of air travel, grand-parents often feel they have little contact with their children and grandchildren because their points of reference are so different. The foci of interest and concern have diverged, and may have moved so far away from each other that it is only with tremendous effort of imagination and will that they enter each other's lives. A woman's mother talks about people in whom her daughter is not interested – school friends long since forgotten, for instance, 'you remember so-and-so, well . . .', and the daughter refers to friends and work colleagues whom the mother has never met. Many reference points for the older woman lie in the past. Her daughter's are concerned with the challenges of the present and future.

A novelist, Nora Kelly, describes it this way, 'People talked about the global village, about how all the different parts of the world were linking up, coming closer together as jets and E-mail and cellular telephones connected everyone everywhere always. Families were stitched together with frequent-flyer bonuses, and friendships kept their health with regular exer-cise of the fax and the answering machine. On the other hand, the points of attachment that fastened each life to others were moving further and further apart, like the universe after the big bang. Her mother's life had been triangulated by New York, Toronto and the farm – manageable distances in her era. Until Gillian had moved West, husband, children, friends, beloved landscapes had all remained within reach. Now mother and daughter lived thousands of miles apart, and Gillian's own points of attachment were stretched across oceans and continents.'[17]

This dislocation may occur even when a mother and daughter are geographically near. A woman moved into her daughter's basement flat, for example, but hated it because she said the children were sent down to say 'hello' to her and see that she was all right, but had no other points of contact with her. She felt that they were simply doing their duty, and she found it humiliating. Just as children sometimes draw a man and woman closer together, but can also prove to be a wedge that drives them apart, children often provide a bridge between a mother's and daughter's lives, but may pull them away from each other, as the younger woman concentrates on the complex tasks and concerns of mothering and the older woman feels out of touch, isolated and perhaps neglected.

Nothing can make up for the lack of shared interests and enthusiasm. When a mother and daughter have plenty to share, they can be many miles apart and yet be close. Equally, when there is nothing over which they collaborate intimacy is spurious, even if they live in the next street.

Self-image

As they become grandmothers women often start to explore the images they have of themselves, both in the present and in the past.

When a daughter has a baby a woman gets a glimpse of how she was herself as a mother twenty or thirty years before. One grandmother says, 'Not since my own children were small have I had the pleasure of cuddling and kissing a baby, cooing and gurgling with him, and glowing with pride at every scrap of progress he makes. I remember being inhibited at expressing these feelings about my own children in public; it wasn't cool to be too obvious about how wonderful they were. But as a granny I don't care.'[18]

A grandmother also compares how she was with her children when they were young with how her daughter or daughter-in-law appears as a mother. She sees herself in minute detail, as if through the wrong end of a telescope. She may realize, for example, that her children missed out on relaxed affection because she was too controlling and anxious. She may get a disturbing picture of herself as rigid and authoritarian – when she had never thought of herself in that way before. Grandmothers see their mothering in a new dimension as they watch their daughters, and thus learn more about themselves.

Becoming a grandmother helps you see who you are now, and what you may be in the future. The jet-setting grandmother, who dreaded getting older, dyes her hair magenta, and reacts to news of her daughter's pregnancy with horror, 'What – me? A *grandmother*? Oh, no!', learns how to accept and love herself as an ageing woman, and gains strength of character, insight and joy through this experience. When her grandchild is placed in her arms, a woman who has endured a loveless marriage rediscovers her capacity for love and a gentleness and softness in herself of which she was not aware. One who has been mourning the death of her partner finds that life opens up again with hope, and confronts the start of each day with renewed vigour. A woman who was determined never to become like her mother, and was locked in conflict with her, realizes that now she is a grandmother she can understand her mother better. A woman whose existence had settled into a tired routine of housework and charity work, entertaining and bridge, finds zest for life, an ability to give and to receive love, and feels reborn. As one grandmother puts it, 'Gradually I have come to incorporate all the conflicting messages about *grandmother* into my own self-image. Now when someone expresses surprise that someone like me (youthful?, attractive?, active?) could be a grandmother, I am able to respond "but this is what a grandmother looks like!"'[19]

To be a lesbian and a grandmother seems almost a contradiction in terms, and lesbian women talking about their experiences as grandmothers may be acutely aware of this. A woman who writes about how she came to reconcile the two images of herself as a grandmother and a lesbian, says that when her daughter became pregnant she began to identify with her in a new way as a woman, but – as with any woman who has been trapped in an unhappy relationship with a man – it brought back disturbing memories of the suffering she went through in her marriage. These were only put to rest when she saw her daughter's tenderness and love for her baby, and came to realize that she, too, had been a loving mother, even in the depths of her misery. 'Imagining our Debbie, my child, as a mother was frightening and depressing to me, but the reality of seeing her as a mother has proved immensely reassuring and healing. Seeing her with her own baby, I have felt a reassurance no words could have given me about the kind of mother I had been.'[20] The baby was a boy and she had to face up to the fact that this male child would grow up to be a man among men – 'the bearers of privilege and the oppressors of women'. She was opposed to the idea of the nuclear family on principle because it isolates and depresses women and children and is 'an inefficient and unjust social organisation'. With the birth of this baby she found herself emotionally invested in just such a family . . . 'Letting go of my fear and anger, I can afford now to make room in my life for my grandson and his father, and to respect them as the family my daughter has chosen for herself.'

Family life is no picnic. A three- or four-generation family may be emotionally warm, with strong friendships, a refuge for those who are especially vulnerable or in need. But even in the happiest of families clan loyalties may be expressed with competing bids for attention and, at times, bitter hostility. A grandmother needs to understand and support without taking sides and without being overwhelmed by the conflict. She develops skills in diplomacy and in lateral thinking. She is wiser.

In fact, when you become a grandmother, it is not that you grow old. It is that you grow up.

Grandmothers on the barricades

It is often claimed that women enjoy being grandmothers because they are not burdened with responsibility. It is true they are not often on twenty-four-hour duty, and can hand a child back to the parents with relief. But a grandmother may feel an awed responsibility for the future and be eager to use her energy to make the world a better and safer place. Becoming a grandmother is a wellspring for political action.

In Argentina the Grandmothers of Plaza de Mayo, founded

in 1977 to try to trace young men and women and their children who had disappeared during 'la represión', march outside the President's Palace in Buenos Aries every week. Many of their grandchildren are still missing and they are determined to find them. The President of this movement is Estela Barnes de Carlotta. Her pregnant daughter, who was active in protesting against the dictatorship, was captured, and immediately after she had given birth she was killed and her baby handed to a couple who supported the regime to bring up as their own. Other children in orphanages were put on display and photographed with placards hanging round their necks announcing, 'I am the daughter of subversives. My parents were killed today.' The anger, tenacity and dedication of these grandmothers makes them a force to be reckoned with. They have succeeded in getting a clause included in the UN Bill of Children's Rights stating that every child has a right to know his or her own identity.[21]

When they started the search for their kidnapped grandchildren they said that the children were like 'war booty' – 'just like they stole the TV, the tape recorder, the radio, the refrigerator'.[22] Now their focus is on recovering identity. The parent–child relationship has to be seen as one element in a broader social context, so they are challenging the proprietary model of children as objects that are owned and of women as breeders.[23]

When women of the grandmother generation demonstrate publicly against tyranny, injustice and war they get headlines in the press, because they are not expected to be radical, to camp out by air bases where weapons of mass destruction stand ready for take-off, as did many grandmothers at Greenham Common, to be incensed at cruelty to animals, at the poisoning of children with toxic fumes, and the ways in which we are wasting the planet.

Middle-aged and elderly women who take part in organized public protests are seen as peculiar. A Conservative newspaper columnist accuses them of being stock characters in 'rent-a-crowd' demonstrations – 'The little old ladies in wheelchairs' . . . 'with slogans for all occasions: disabled rallies, "anti-nazi" rallies and anti-motorway campaigns.'[24] No one is surprised when the young are angry. But to be middle-aged – even old – and angry raises eyebrows, especially if you are educated, comfortably off and socially respectable. Grandmothers are supposed to be gentle, not fierce, conforming, not rebellious, placid rather than challenging.

Under communism grandmothers had immense importance. Since all young women worked outside the home, grandmothers cared for the children. As Nina, a Czech grandmother explains, 'What was outside the family was not important. Nobody had any influence on it, anyway. The Communist Party took charge of everything. So what was left was pleasure from the grandchildren. This was the only treasure the family had, and it could not be stolen.'

When communism was destroyed grandmothers became less important because mothers of young children stayed at home. The grandmother was redundant, and she was often very poor, living on an inadequate pension. Nina believes that grandmothers still have an important task of moral guidance, because the new freedom has brought with it new problems. 'We have to learn how to lead our lives by ourselves. There is a lack of responsibility among the young. There is a new brutality.' In a society which has undergone revolution the grandmother is a constant symbol of enduring principles, giving to others without asking for reward, committed to clear ideas of right and wrong and embodying the supreme value of love. In any culture in which values have changed dramatically the grandmother becomes a moral icon in social and political life.

In northern and western countries an increasing number of grandmothers are not content to be symbols – they actively seek social change. Because they want their children and their children's children to survive in a world in which their limbs are not blown off by land-mines, which is not choking on its excrement and where trees and wild flowers still grow, a world which is free from racial hatred and from war, they become politically active.

This is not a new phenomenon. Rabbi Julia Neuberger says of her father's mother, an Orthodox upper-middle-class woman, who in 1933 staged one-woman sit-ins on the Home Office steps to demand visas for Jewish children trapped in Germany for whom she could find homes in England, 'It may sound extraordinary, but I believe she was liberated by the refugee crisis. Large numbers of her own family . . . were still in Germany, and she battled to get them out.'[25]

Yes, there are grandmothers who are content to knit bootees and shawls, to give presents, baby-sit occasionally, and have their grandchildren for a meal once a week. But in the world today thousands upon thousands of grandmothers have been politicized by the experience of bearing and rearing children and seeing them in their turn bearing children in a world which is sordid, polluted and violent. As a result, they have new insight, fresh energy, and are committed to joining with others in order to change the society in which they live.

Looking after granny

You are full of vigour, fit and sparkling. But you realize that you cannot depend on being like this for ever. Growing older brings new challenges and it is wise to think ahead to the changes that need to happen if your health starts to fail. How is it going to affect your children and your grandchildren? What can you do to plan in advance so that daughters and daughters-in-law (because it is almost invariably women who have to shoulder these responsibilities) do not feel torn between their own children's needs and your demands on them? A woman who is 65 years old today has, on average, a life expectancy of 18 years, and will probably be healthy and active for at least 10 of those years.[26] But the chances are that after that time she will begin to lose her sight (with glaucoma, cataract or diabetes) or need a hearing aid. Although these health problems can be treated, she requires help with ordinary, everyday tasks. Half of all women have had a fracture of the pelvis, wrist or spine by the age of seventy as a consequence of osteoporosis, which makes bones brittle.[27] Knees and hands may get stiff with arthritis, too, and muscles are weaker than in middle age. Going up and down stairs and using public transport may be difficult. For some women it also brings memory loss, and for an unlucky minority, Alzheimer's.

Increasing numbers of women, having delayed motherhood until they are in their late thirties, are burdened with simultaneously trying to care for young children and elderly parents, often with commitments to work outside the home as well, either paid or voluntary. As they find it an impossible task, they begin to feel stressed and guilty. A grandmother may not understand how every hour of her daughter's life is crammed with things that she has to do, not just soon but *now*. If she is out of touch with her children's and grandchildren's lives she may feel socially isolated, rejected by her family, and angry and self-pitying about this. Many couples come to the point when they have to ask, 'What on earth do we do with Mother?' It may be impossible for a daughter or daughter-in-law to make space in her busy life to get to granny's house to do her laundry or fix a meal for her, or even to pop in to the granny flat across the hall at a time when she is expected. Unless helpers are available, the only alternatives may be either to move into special accommodation for the elderly where this help is part of the service, or to settle on a 'home'.

Few governments provide adequate care for the elderly disabled. If a grandmother is to stay in her own home, efficient, caring home help services are vital. Denmark is a remarkable exception. There the home help services are financed and provided by local government and available to *all* older people free of charge. In Germany, free home help is restricted to those on welfare or who have recently been in hospital. Only ten per cent of the elderly in the UK have a home help service.[28]

It is unrealistic to ignore the fact that when we are over seventy-five ageing is likely to reduce mobility. How are we going to cope with it? However much our children love us, they may not be able to handle our problems at the same time as they are struggling to be good parents, and dealing with the inevitable crises of child-rearing. If you hope to live into your eighties, it makes sense to plan ahead, to explore alternative arrangements for housing and care.

Our own
Grandmothers

W hat kind of grandmother do you aim to be? It may have something to do with how you remember your own grandmothers.

A strong theme runs through much of the feminist discourse about grandmothers – a celebration of our grandmothers as women who toiled, suffered, endured and conquered – and the literature emanating from some feminist publishing houses occasionally borders on the mystic. It must be difficult for any woman who considers herself a feminist to confess that she disliked her maternal grandmother (for it is invariably the mother's mother who is honoured) or that she had little in common with her.

In reality, of course, not all grandmothers were noble, wise, or even loving. Journalist and 'enfant terrible' Julie Burchill claims that her grandmother encouraged her to play truant from school with her cousins whenever possible and to go shoplifting for her under pain of a white-hot poker.[1] 'Naturally we loved her above all others.' The exceptions leap from the pages with refreshing candour. Margaret Atwood, for example, seems to speak with autobiographical authenticity when she describes a fictional character's relationship with her grandmother, a hard disciplinarian who used to lock the little girl in the coal cellar as a punishment. She writes of the terror a small child felt then:

> I'm holding my grandmother around both legs, but I didn't think of them as legs, I thought of her as one solid piece from the neck down to the bottom of her skirt. I feel as if I'm holding on to the edge of something, safety, if I let go I'll fall, I want forgiveness, but she's prying my hands away finger by finger. She's smiling; she was proud of the fact that she never lost her temper. I know I will be shut in the cellar by myself. I'm afraid of that . . . Sometimes there were things down there, I could hear

them moving around, small things that might get on you and run up your legs. I, crying because I'm afraid, can't stop, and even if I hadn't done anything wrong I'd still be put down there, for making noise, for crying. 'Laugh and the world laughs with you,' said my grandmother. *'Cry and you cry alone.'*

Later she adds,

'I used to pray that I wouldn't live long enough to get like my grandmother.'[2]

Some grandmothers are remembered with outright horror, like the one who always had her mouth open, 'mauve tongue cracked down the centre from seven decades of use, disappearing into cavernous blackness beyond'.

That voice, screaming repartee at her powder-blue parakeet Bootsie . . . 'You're late!' she'd bellow into the phone to my parents who used to drop my sister and me at her apartment for a few terrifying hours every few weeks. There, by the tea table, under the embroidered portrait of three cats in dresses jumping into a lily pond, among the white ceramic figurines of shepherdesses and swans in eighteenth-century dress, Granny reigned. She bought us colouring books, but wouldn't let us do the colouring in. We sat idly by, watching her neatly fill in Bambi, Cinderella or Lady and the Tramp.

When one of these granddaughters married she presided at the reception 'like a great jewelled frog in green satin'. Not long after, she was buried in the same green satin, and her granddaughter, kneeling to pray by the corpse, could not understand why she looked so different, until she realized that, at last, the mouth was closed.[3]

I knew only one of my grandmothers; I had to rely on my mother's memories to learn about her own mother. But I saw my father's mother two or three times a week, and I remember feeling sorry for her. She was a tall, gaunt woman, with pepper-and-salt hair, wire glasses, a gauze scarf at her neck and button-up shoes, who passed her time playing the piano with bony fingers and at games of bridge with other grannies. Her world was circumscribed, fear-ridden and self-centred. She was alarmed by the thunder storms that I loved and angry when I picked the daffodils in the little garden she had told me could be my own.

It was so difficult to explain things to her, so hard to get her to understand. She could not see how unjust I thought her actions were, nor comprehend the thrill of thunder and lightning. There was a gulf between us. Looking back on it, I now see that she was probably very lonely and longed to be accepted as a friend by her only son's wife, but had no idea how to be one. I felt no affinity with her.

Yet most women who described their grandmothers to me remember them with great fondness and feel a powerful bond with them. You may get some idea of what you can give your grandchildren if you had a grandmother whom you loved and think about what it was in her that you most valued. You can talk with other women about how they remember their grandmothers, too, and about their relationships with those who are still alive.

Special food

When women describe their grandmothers, food is a recurrent theme: the garlicky smells of grandma's kitchen, the shining rows of bottled peaches and apple sauce in her pantry, the taste of gingerbread still warm from the oven, or the lollipops she gave as a reward for good behaviour. The broadcaster Gloria Hunniford has assembled a book of her Irish grandmother's recipes. She recalls,

> Granny McCann lived on a farm, and all my best memories are of spending lots of time with her through the long, hot summers until the hay was brought in. Everything was done by hand; the hay had to be pitched with a fork and once it had all been loaded, we'd jump on the back of the wagon and hitch a ride home. My grandmother was a very large woman and I'll always remember her appearing through a haze of

heat, a wicker basket lined with gingham on her hip, with cups of strong tea and soda farls – flat triangular shapes cooked on a griddle and very special to Ireland. They'd be covered with melting butter and home-made preserves. Within minutes the butter and fresh damson jam would be running down your chin. I'm lucky enough to have eaten in some of the best restaurants in the world but I can tell you now nothing ever tasted as good as Granny McCann's griddle bread.[4]

For families who have been uprooted and dispersed to different countries, or fragmented by genocide, grandmothers represent the continuity of a cultural tradition that might otherwise be forgotten. They have always had an important role in retaining cultural identity through food. My mother, who hated cooking, learned how to make Scottish drop scones on her mother-in-law's iron girdle; it was an acknowledgement of the values of courage, thrift and hard work which had enabled my father's poor crofter grandparents to survive in a harsh environment. When he taught me how to make potato scones, first testing the heat of the girdle with flour and a goose feather, and how porridge should be eaten with salt, not sugar, with the milk in a separate bowl, it was never just a matter of whether food like this was good to eat – rather the privilege of being initiated into a strong cultural tradition, and becoming part of the family tree. When I make potato scones for my grandchild I pass on that tradition and preserve that identity, even if in a much diluted form.

Women recall the smells and tastes of a Polish grandmother's chicken soup and *kugel*, a Russian grandmother's stuffed cabbage and bortsch, huge Italian spaghetti dinners, and home-made bread, blackberry jelly and blueberry or rhubarb wines. 'She used to give me mashed potato with chicken soup poured over it says a Canadian woman of her Jewish grandmother. 'No one else has ever served me that.'

Though some cookery-book writers never mention their grandmothers' cooking because their childhood was lived in a gastronomic wasteland, others refer fondly to dishes they relished as children. These grandmothers' recipes crop up among sophisticated recipes for Californian, French, Italian or the latest 'nouvelle cuisine'. 'This recipe is one my Nan used to serve on washday Mondays to go with the inevitable cold Sunday joint leftovers,' writes a chef famous for his exotic vegetable concoctions, introducing herbed potato scones.[5] It is as if they want to acknowledge a debt to the women who, as children, they watched slaving away in the kitchen, and then dishing up meals with pride, and yearn to reinforce their personal link with family and cultural tradition.

A grandmother's prejudices and dogmas about diet sometimes push a grandchild into longing to savour the opposite. The distinguished food writer M F K Fisher said she owed a great deal to her grandmother's 'Nervous Stomach'. The family used to relish the times when grandma went off on her periodic visits to spas to drink sea water and have colonic irrigation, for it was only then that they could eat what they liked, enjoy their food, talk about it and relax together. 'Here am I, . . . at least ninety-five years after my maternal grandmother first abandoned herself to the relatively voluptuous fastings and lavages of a treatment for the fashionable disorder, blaming or crediting it for the fact that I have written several books about gastronomy, a subject that my ancestor would have saluted, if at all, with a refined but deep-down belch of gastric protest.' She goes on to say, 'If my grandmother had not been blessed with her "nervous stomach" I might never have realized that breaking bread together can be nourishing to more than the body . . .'[6]

The gift of food represents love. This can be important to a small child: the special biscuits that you cook together, the buttery, light seed-cake, and the trifle with sponge-cake soaked in sherry, piled with whipped cream and topped with cherries, that I can remember from my own childhood. They bring evocative memories of a grandmother's love.

There is a temptation to romanticize the foods of memory, however, and imagine that grandmothers worked skilfully and effortlessly in the kitchen, suffused with pleasure in a service to which they were devoted because of their love for us. It does not always work out like that. My own mother hated cooking and thought it was a waste of time. So when her five little granddaughters came to stay she fed them on cold rice pudding straight from the can. My father varied the diet with heated-up cans of baked beans and slippery, sloppy spaghetti in tomato sauce of a particularly virulent red. They loved staying there and, indeed, cold rice pudding had about it something of an exotic tinge, both because they adored their grandparents and because the diet in that house was completely different from the carefully balanced meals with fresh vegetables and fruit that they had at home.

Things that a child may see as powerful accomplishments may be, at best, repetitive chores and, at worst, virtual kitchen slavery for a grandmother. The Indian novelist, Shashi Deshpande, tells how she suddenly realized this from a casual remark made by her husband's mother as she showed her calloused palms and said with 'neither complaint nor self-pity in her tone, "I used to make fifty to sixty *bhakris* (a flat, dry bread) every morning. Sometimes, I think I was born only for this." Coming from a prosaic, matter-of-fact woman who never spoke of "Life", nor indeed of any generalities, it was an astonishing statement . . . As if the focus had shifted, my vision suddenly changed. And instead of that safe, warm haven of my childhood, I saw another kitchen, where the women were chained to endless, tedious labour, crouching for hours before a smoking fire. Accompanying this picture were no pleasant sounds, but the angry orchestra women beat out on pots and pans.'[7]

Sometimes women remember their grandmothers with a fear that is relieved only by memories of the special pies or cakes they baked. It is sad that for some grandmothers their only link with a child is through food, and that this should remain the isolated positive memory in an adult grandchild's mind. A woman who as a small child was very afraid of her stern grandmother, who never expressed her emotions and was unable to communicate love, said, 'Everything always seemed dark. Her house was dark. Her clothing was dark. I always wondered why no one opened up the windows. We had to be quiet when we saw her. But she gave me chocolates, and I had the feeling she kept those chocolates for me and no one else. It was gloomy and scary until the chocolates came out. I knew they were in a golden metallic box on the top of the fridge just for me! That made me feel special – that she would make the effort to buy them with me in mind and then keep them in the box waiting for my visits.'

A gift of love in the form of food does not compensate for the absence of love expressed in other ways.

Playthings and cherished things

Thinking back to their childhood, adults can often describe in detail the presents given by their grandparents. It seems to be an expected part of the grandmother role that she comes bearing gifts. These are often playthings which are too expensive for parents to afford.

But they are sometimes inappropriate, and often there are too many of them. One woman says of her husband's mother, 'She brings toys every visit, and we are inundated with bloody toys. But despite "nice" requests to stop, they keep coming! We've started donating them to a charity!'

It can be a difficult task getting a small child to show appreciation of a toy and thank granny when he's clearly more interested in the box in which it came, or when a boy who really wanted a doll of his own was presented with a truck, or a girl is given yet another doll when she would have much preferred a construction set. It is worth discussing with a daughter or daughter-in-law the kind of playthings right for a child's particular developmental stage, and those which, perhaps, parents cannot afford, but which you can give on some special occasion. But gifts do not have to be expensive. Cheap toys are often remembered long after more expensive ones are forgotten. One woman's intense memory of her grandmother is of her laughing as she was taking photographs of children all blowing bubbles from the pipes she had just given them.

Adults often remember vividly things that were never intended to be playthings, but were objects in a grandmother's house which were special: the writing desk with a secret drawer, her jewellery box – glittering with paste brooches and rings – the slatted picture which from one angle is a garden, from another a woman in a straw bonnet with a bouquet of flowers, the china dog on the mantelpiece whose head wobbled up and down, or a snowstorm in a glass globe. One woman remembers a ballet doll in a bottle; you switched a key and the dancer turned, 'I wasn't allowed to touch it but my nanna would play it over and over again for me.' Another remembers the pleasure of looking at the wine glasses in her grandmother's crystal cabinet. This grandmother also collected clocks, 'When we arrived she would make her clocks chime in every room.' I have an intense memory myself of the scent of my grandmother's stone-flagged pantry and the delicacy of the muslin covers, each one over its bowl of cream or jug of milk, from which were suspended bright blue beads which seemed to me as a child utterly beautiful.

The stuff of memories

Each of us brings special aptitudes to grandmotherhood: telling an exciting story, helping a child to write, read, to arithmetic or learn a foreign language, playing chess, finding out about the past, or we may simply be good at playing and giving cuddles. Like many other women talking about loved grandmothers, a woman remembers the delights of sharing with her grandmother 'going shopping, reading, singing, dressing up, dinner times, sleeping in the big beds, holidays in the country, being cuddled, doing housework, looking at photos of my parents when they were young, and listening to stories of what they used to get up to – and a big comfy lap to crawl in to.' Another says, 'I enjoyed staying at her house and sleeping in her bed. She would cuddle me to sleep. I thought her breasts were softer than pillows.' As the girl grew, 'I talked to her with my problems and she would tell me hers.' She goes on to saying, 'Remembering this, I feel sad' – and she is in tears, grieving over her much loved grandmother who has now died. Another woman, both of whose grandmothers are dead, says of them, 'They were around whenever needed and gave lots of love and caring. I miss my grandmothers very much, especially with the birth of my own daughters. It is sad that they didn't get to hold them and pass on their love to them. I truly would love to see them again for a kiss and a big hug.' Some grandmothers find it difficult to express themselves in physical affection. A woman describes her grandmother,

> The language of touch so foreign to my family, caused my grandmother to stiffen like the starched shirts of

the young boys in the country schools . . . Even now if I were to see her, it would be in poorest taste to speak of affection. But the ivory-coloured Afghan she sent at Christmas whispers love from the rocker each time I pass.[8]

When a grandmother has died the birth of children often makes parents feel that there is a hole in the family – that a special quality of love is missing which they had found in the grandmother. And they grieve afresh. 'There was a lot of love and warmth in her house. I miss my little Nan and would have loved her to meet my boys,' a very young mother writes. Her grandmother had given her security and understanding through her troubled teenage years. She goes on to say, as her writing becomes erratic and tear-stained, 'I am sorry this is such a mess, but I am quite upset now.'

A perceptive grandmother who has tolerance and sympathy for the turbulence of adolescence often provides sanctuary and peace to a confused teenager. Women describe 'just talking to my grandmother, particularly on summer evenings in her garden until quite late', 'She gave us love, support and a sense of belonging. She accepted us as we were.' A woman says her grandmother was 'assertive, but never bossy, and never judgemental. I was always close to her. As a teenager I found a good friend in my grandmother. I could talk to her and she listened, whereas my mum was always too busy. She was my best friend.' 'I used to feel sorry for people that didn't have their grandmothers living with them,' another woman says. 'She was always there for me when I was growing up, and throughout my teenage years. We used to sit or lie on her bed together, talking about all kinds of things, but mostly about people and relationships. I have so many important memories of her that I could write a book. I still love my Nan as much now as when she was alive.' This grandmother suffered from Alzheimer's in her old age. 'A few days before she died she became lucid and asked me if I was going to be all right when she was gone . . . I find it hard to think of her without crying, but at the same time I feel blessed that I had such a special relationship with such a wonderful person.' Another woman was bored by a grandmother who spent years of her life 'bombed out of her mind by excess medication', but once free of those drugs 'she was mentally reborn. I enjoyed learning to talk to her woman-to-woman. My pregnancy gave us a real point of contact, and holding her long-awaited great-grandson in her arms was the happiest moment she had had for many years.' She died when the baby was six months old.

Grandmothers weave a family story. They link the present and future with the past, and the oral histories they tell are an important part of a family's sense of its own being, and of each individual's identity within it. When there is no grandmother, or when she prefers to treat the past as a closed book because it is painful for her to talk about it, and remembers only the tragedy and none of the comedy, or when she has made off to a condominium for the over fifty-fives in Florida, and grandchildren visit for a fun-packed vacation once a year, there is often no one to take that place.

As you become a grandmother yourself you see your own grandmother in a new way. It may be only then that you feel kinship with her. A woman who, as a child, was frightened of her grandmother writes,

> skin of wax, hair of silk
> legs of polished lumber
> hand veins of blue ribbons
>
> you were the crone, hag, witch
> that folklore is made of.
> now you are my sister.[9]

Across generations, across history, bridging all differences, you share the experience of being a grandmother.

Other Grandmothers

Grandmothers in traditional cultures

In most traditional cultures grandmothers are people of immense importance and authority, and a woman never really acquires power until she becomes a grandmother. In an Arab harem the husband's mother controls the lives of all the women within it. A Moroccan, describing her childhood says, 'Opposite the men's salon was the august space occupied by my paternal grandmother, Lalla Mani (*lalla* is a female term of respect in Arabic). Because my grandfather was dead, my grandmother was the symbolic head of the harem. She was a constitutional monarch; in a way she was like the Queen. The heads of the family were my uncle and father, my uncle being slightly more important because he was the first-born son. But they had to consult with my grandmother on every family decision, such as schooling or an upcoming marriage – or even a party at the house. Lalla Mani gave me the sense that women could reach the top, and that's one thing we have lost with the dwindling of the extended family. We have no older role models in Morocco now.'[1]

When you become a grandmother you attain dignity and authority as a matriarch, can speak as an elder and pass on the cultural traditions of your people through your daughters or daughters-in-law. It is a peak point in your life. In tribal societies you may have religious functions, too. In many South African villages the chief grandmother tends the sacred fire which must be kept burning at all times, and if a new village is built it is she who ritually lights the ceremonial fire.

In some cultures being a grandmother does not depend on your own children having children. In Thailand, for example, you are called 'grandmother' when any younger relative has a baby. The grandmother role is not tied to reproductive status.[2] The Chinese veneration for old people is well known. A son's most important obligation is to ensure that his parents have a happy and comfortable old age, and elderly people are afforded something approaching reverence. In the traditional Japanese family, fertility and particularly the birth of sons was so important that if a couple had no male heirs to carry on the family name, to tend the ancestral tablets when they died, as well as to look after them in old age, they adopted a boy, often a brother's son, and brought him up as their own. In Japan, too, virtually every old person became a grandparent.[3]

In harsh conditions among nomadic people, who must keep on the move, the elderly, the weak and the very young are a liability. A woman who has just had a baby must get in the saddle and be ready to ride again. A feeble old person who cannot keep up with the others is left behind in Arctic conditions to die of hypothermia. But in settled agricultural societies the old are cherished, even in poverty. In Fiji I was told, 'We don't leave our parents away. We stay close, in the same house or surrounding. We share. What is mine is yours. What is yours mine.'

Age is respected throughout Africa. Among the Kgatla of Botswana couples start their married life in the home of either the husband's or the wife's parents, and are subject to the authority of the head of that household. If it is your parents' house your husband must visit stealthily at night. If it is your husband's parents' home you must be submissive and behave like a servant in the house. In both cases the grandmother controls everything that goes on in the domestic sphere. In pregnancy your mother advises you how to look after yourself, and she cares for you in childbirth. When wives go to live in the man's mother's compound they are trained and tested by her and it is her job to help them be good mothers and to oversee the welfare of her grandchildren. Grandmothers maintain this supervisory role, if they are able, into old age and until the day of their death.[4]

Married sons have a responsibility to assist their parents with ploughing, give them presents occasionally and assist in any way they can. Married daughters help in the household and make gifts of food and clothing. There is great emphasis on honouring and obeying parents, and young people consult them before embarking on any new venture or coming to any important decision. A Kgatla grandmother has great dignity, and a continuing stake in your children's and grandchildren's progress and welfare.

In tribal South Africa a woman usually goes back to her grandmother's home to give birth. It is considered the safest place, both because the ancestors dwell there and because a woman's grandmother is likely to be past the menopause, so that the home will be uncontaminated by menstrual blood.[5] The grandmother, as well as a woman's own mother or her husband's mother, is present at birth. Afterwards the new mother is in seclusion with her baby, tended by her mother (among the Pedi, Xhosa and Sotho) or husband's mother (among the Zulu) until post-partum bleeding has stopped. Nurturing and education of the new mother by the older woman used to last much longer in the past – often until the baby was three years old. Today, especially in urban areas, the grandmother's immediate responsibility lasts only until the baby's umbilical cord stump drops off. It is difficult for new mothers because husbands hardly ever help with looking after the baby or with household chores.[6]

On outlying islands of Fiji, where there is a well-organized modern health care system, I found from interviews with the midwives and women in 1995, that some women having first babies, and most of those having second or subsequent ones, still choose to give birth in their own or their mother's home with a midwife and help from their mothers and other older women. It is considered shameful for a woman to be forced to give birth without women of the family to support her. If she is in hospital alone they have failed her at a critical time in her life, 'When you give birth your mother must be at your side.' The maternal grandmother supervises the pregnancy, encourages exercise, and mixes special herbs to make bush tea which the expectant mother drinks to 'make the baby fresh', to relieve discomforts of pregnancy and, if she is overdue, to bring on labour. Often it is the maternal grandmother who massages the new mother's uterus with coconut oil and baths the baby, and she cooks the meals and looks after the other children in the days following, and arranges the ceremony of 'the stopping of the blood' when the mother emerges from seclusion.

Korean birth traditions, like those of other pre-industrial cultures, are based on the family. An important function exercised by a midwife is to help integrate the mother and baby into her husband's family. The mother-in-law is responsible for preparing her son's wife for childbirth and it is believed that her actions and spirit influence the baby's character while it is still developing in the uterus, so it is important that there is harmony and peace in the home. She should offer her daughter-in-law delicious and beautifully presented dishes, create lovely surroundings for her, and do everything she can to ensure her happiness. She assists during labour, giving back and abdominal massage which includes a slapping movement, and also offers prayers to Samshin, the Goddess of Birth. Once the baby is born she cooks the traditional meal of rice and seaweed soup for the new mother. She makes sure that the new mother can rest and eat well, keeps the house quiet, clean, well-ordered and welcoming for the baby and leaves the mother and baby alone so that they have time together to get to know each other. She gives offerings to Samshin and prays that the mother will have plenty of breast milk.[7]

In most cultures grandmothers take an active part in caring for and educating grandchildren. Along with a woman's sisters or sisters-in-law (depending on where the family home is), cousins and aunts, she is fully involved from the moment a baby is born. In Japan, for instance, where grandparents often live in the same small house as children and grandchildren, with only rice-paper screens dividing the rooms, they may have a grandchild sleeping with them. In fact, if there is little space the whole family may sleep in the same room. The Western custom of sleeping alone is not part of traditional Japanese culture.

In some societies a woman may be given a grandchild to rear. Children are often sent to their grandmother's house to be finally weaned from the breast, though by that time they are often three years old or more. They return after a while, or may stay there till they are grown up.

Grandmothers sometimes breastfeed their grandchildren if a mother has died or is ill and relactate when they are themselves past child-bearing. As she gets older a strong grandchild will run errands, carry firewood and water, and be her eyes and ears. This is not like sending a child to live in isolation with an elderly person. A child is a child of the extended family, and the mother–child relationship is not exclusive. The grandmother herself is part of a close-knit community and everyone, not only family members, plays a part in the children's lives. A Hawaiian maternal grandmother has the right to choose a child her daughter bears, to rear as her own. A child may also be given to a barren sister or cousin who asks for a baby. There is an established practice of surrogacy. In parts of West Africa any senior woman in the extended family may ask a woman of subordinate social status for a child once weaning is completed, or takes over breastfeeding the child herself. Among the Fulani it is believed that when a woman is pregnant her milk belongs to the baby inside her, so she should stop breast-feeding, and there is a special heat that comes from her uterus which can make an older child ill with diarrhoea, fever and weight loss. So another woman – often the paternal grandmother who lives in the same house – takes over the care of the older sibling. In households where several women are pregnant at the same time a grandmother may be responsible for a brood of grandchildren who eat and sleep with her.[8] Whereas in northern countries it is difficult for couples over the age of forty to adopt or for women to get fertility treatment, because there is a general assumption that mothers must be young if they are to cope with a child, in traditional societies, on the contrary, older women have an active role in the day-to-day lives of babies and older children.

All the work of child care, as well as of caring for men and for the elderly, is shared between women, and a strong female support network is built through these shared responsibilities and concerns. Their lives are intermeshed in complex patterns.

The powerful emotional bonds between mothers and daughters and daughters and grandmothers among the Ndembu of Zambia, a matrilineal society, grow from early childhood, for children are reared in their maternal grandmother's home from the age of three or four until just before puberty.[9] The importance of maternal grandmothers is expressed in Ndembu religion; mother and maternal grandmother ghosts often visit women, whereas ghosts of the husband's mother and grandmother hardly ever put in an appearance. The spirits of a mother and a grandmother who have died are invoked when there is infertility because it is believed that they guard the entry to the uterus and are preventing the woman from conceiving. Only when they have been propitiated will they help her have a baby. In the ceremony of Nkang'a, the girls' puberty ritual, the young girl is taken away from her mother in order to go off and produce grandchildren, and at the end of the rite the novice is led to her grandmother's hut before she is taken to her bridegroom for the wedding night. The rite expresses the girl's separation from her maternal lineage so that she can go out, have children, and then return them to the lineage of which her maternal grandmother is the senior representative.

In some native North American societies, too, grandmothers have great authority. The maternal grandmother is head of the Hopi household, which usually consists of a woman, her daughters, their husbands and any unmarried sons and daughters. Your son calls your home, rather than the home he shares with his wife, his own. On feast days he always comes home to you and later, after your death, he goes to his sister's, while his wife continues to celebrate feasts in her mother's home. In a similar way the Navajo have what has been called 'matrilocal grand-families'.[10] When a couple marry they can live either with the husband's or the wife's mother, but the pull is always stronger to her mother. The grandparents decide such matters as when sheep should be dipped or sheared, and are the final authority on all matters concerning agriculture. A Navajo grandmother does not impose her decisions. Instead, she is the centre of the web of communication and organizes everyone so that they co-operate.[11] She does not need to work *through* men, but has a political role as a mediator *between* them.

In Atjeh, on the northern tip of Sumatra, women own the houses, and even though men may own land, women work it. They grow rice, which is the staple food, and the essential ingredient for sacrificial rites, so no man can sacrifice to the gods without the women's co-operation. The tie between a mother and her children and grandchildren is the most powerful in the community, and husbands are treated as guests who often outstay their welcome. Approximately 50 per cent of all marriages end in divorce.[12]

In ex-slave societies the importance of the grandmother is reinforced in conditions of urban poverty. Poor black American households often consist of a three-generational unit made up of a woman, one or more of her daughters, her daughters' children, and any men with whom the women may be living. Women with children may have no alternative but to live with their mothers and share resources, and unemployed sons live with their mothers for the same reason.

Grandmothers are powerful throughout the Caribbean, and often rear their grandchildren from the time they are weaned. In Jamaica the tradition is that a peasant woman does not expect to marry until she has established a long and fertile relationship with a man who provides for her and her children. So when you are middle-aged you usually have children of your own living at home together with your daughters' children, and bring them up together. Although they grumble about this, grandmothers like to have strong, healthy children around as they get older. They run errands, fetch water and firewood, help in the house, with horticultural work, and with 'higgling' (selling market produce). As the grandmother gets older the girls gradually take over more and more responsibility for the running of the household, and by old age a woman expects granddaughters to be caring for her in their turn. It is considered a dreadful thing to leave elderly women without young people to help them. When I was doing my fieldwork I met grandmothers who proudly claimed that sons who were emigrating had deliberately made their girlfriends pregnant so that there would be a baby to leave with their mothers when they went abroad. In these cases women whose daughters had not given them grandchildren were rearing their sons' children.

When a young woman becomes pregnant her mother will not 'quarrel' provided there is a man to 'response' for the baby. He does not have to marry her, but must accept some financial obligation. If there is no man to do this the girl may be flogged and turned out of the house. Maternal relatives then intercede with the grandmother to allow her daughter home again, which she usually does after a while. The baby used to be born in the grandmother's house, and the woman cared for him with the help of her mother for nine months to a year, after which time she went off to seek work in the town, leaving the baby with her mother. The pattern is similar to that of the Ndembu. A young woman goes out from her mother's house to get children to bring back and give to her mother. The flogging and turning out constitute a transitional ritual to mark a woman's passage to motherhood, a ceremony in which she, as it were, 'pays' for the right to sexuality and motherhood.

In Guiana men do not have much authority, not only in their

homes, but also in other spheres of economic and political life, whereas mothers and grandmothers are acknowledged as strong. A child born to a daughter living at home often grows up calling the grandmother 'Mama' and addresses his mother by her first name, as if she were a sister, especially if the grandmother has young children of her own as well. A grandmother treats her children and grandchildren exactly the same. She is the family boss.[13] But when children and grandchildren are not brought up together grandmothers treat their grandchildren with affectionate indulgence.[14] They take their sides in arguments with their mothers. When a young girl wants to go to a dance, for example, and her mother forbids it, the grandmother often intercedes for her.

This raises an interesting point about grandmothers. In most societies there is a general belief that women indulge their grandchildren and do not discipline them enough, and are so lenient that they can 'get away with murder'. Anthropologists call it the 'equivalence of generations', meaning that individuals belonging to alternate generations behave towards each other in a more relaxed way than those in consecutive generations.

All over the world grandparents and grandchildren joke with each other in a way which parents and children rarely do. Grandchildren can tease or disobey their grandparents without being punished. But a grandmother who cossets her grandchildren may at the same time be authoritarian, sometimes even tyrannical, with her daughters-in-law. In Taiwan young women living with their mothers-in-law have a high suicide rate.[15] On the other hand, though a lot of bickering goes on between them, especially regarding the disciplining of the children, having her mother-in-law on hand means that a daughter-in-law is free to go and visit her own parents, as she always has help with the children. Women criticise their daughters-in-law for punishments which they consider too harsh, even though they may have punished their own children in a similar way.

Taiwanese grandmothers are busy with match-making, even planning who the children will marry when they grow up. Daughters-in-law tolerate this, realising that grandma is unlikely to be still around when these decisions have to be made. Grandmothers visit from house to house in pursuit of their plans and act as paid intermediaries between families. They also arrange adoptions, settle family disputes, and negotiate face-saving compromises in quarrels.[16] At family ceremonies there is great expenditure of woman-power, and grandmothers are very active at birthdays, weddings, funerals and religious festivals. Younger women draw on their grandmothers' experiences, who record exactly how a big family ceremony was celebrated last time and the time before that, and all the other times within living memory. Some grandmothers become known as the wise women of the community, and are consulted by others in the village on matters relating to family, marriage and child-rearing. They also dominate the short-term loan associations, from which families borrow in order to have enough money to arrange a wedding or funeral. They do a little business, too, selling their chickens and ducks to neighbours or in the market, and may become money-lenders at a high rate of interest. A favourite occupation of grandmothers, especially those who were formally prostitutes, is gambling at mah-jong or cards, and it can be a major concern of the family to keep granny from gambling away the family savings.

But grandmothers are also very active in religious functions. They go on tours around religious centres, combining sightseeing with worship of the gods. When temples are restored grandmothers raise money for repairs and organize the celebrations. Religious festivals are linked with outdoor opera or puppet shows, and older women sit for long hours watching both afternoon and evening performances. Apparently the most successful programmes on Taiwanese television are these lengthy opera and puppet shows, and an anthropologist says that interviewing was impossible at any time when one of these programmes was being screened.[16]

Traditionally, when a Japanese grandmother enters the last and oldest age-group, at the age of sixty-one, there is a party. From now on she must be treated with great consideration. Everything she asks for must be given her, her opinions listened to with respect, and she must never be criticized. For the first time since childhood she can wear red clothes. In recognition of having attained the full status of an *oba-san* she dons a crimson underskirt. Old age is not a disability which a person tries to ignore, but a triumph, and a vantage point attained at last at the end of the long road of child-rearing.

Today, in some northern cultures there are women who strive to regain their self-confidence upon becoming older and their dignity as grandmothers. The 'grand' in 'grandmother' derives from a Latin word which means 'impressive', 'important', 'powerful' and 'strong'. In the United States of America groups of Jewish women, for instance, enact the ceremony of *Simhat lochmah*, the celebration of wisdom, traditionally a rite restricted to men. In this celebration a woman, in the company of female friends, carries the Torah, representing the wisdom of the people, and is given a new name that acknowledges her new status. Women are reclaiming the 'grand' in being grandmothers.

Grandmothers in myth and the Grandmother Goddess

It is not surprising that, given the importance of grandmothers in traditional societies, they appear as powerful figures in myth and legend. There is Muriranga-whenua who gave to the Maori people her jaw-bone, the bone of enchantment and of knowledge, and Eve, in Jewish and Christian faith, the first woman and hence the grandmother of humanity, who picked the apple of knowledge of good and evil and gave it to man to eat. Legends also tell how the grandmother of a tribe first made and fired pots, essential to carry water and contain food, or invented the art of cooking to feed her hungry people. The Hawaiian goddess Pele manifests herself in the form of an old woman. Her name is Tutu, which means 'grandmother'.

Because they are so powerful, grandmothers in myth and legend are often dangerous. Muriranga-whenua used to eat her grandchildren until the hero of the Maori nation tricked her and she gave him her jaw-bone as a reward for his audacity. Hidden inside Red Riding Hood's grandmother there was a wolf.

Grandmothers are honoured for the experience and wisdom they represent. They are a vital link – perhaps the last surviving one – in the ancestral chain and hence the origins of the tribe or clan. They can remember the myths and legends, and recount the story of the past. But even more than this, the archetypal figure of the grandmother embodies the power of the earth and of nature. She is the great Grandmother Goddess.

Goddesses are often thought of as beautiful maidens, but this is just one image of the goddess. One of her earliest forms was as the moon, and the moon's phases were also phases in the life of a mother. 'The crescent moon was a young girl, the maiden; the full moon was the pregnant woman, the mother; the darkening moon was the wise old woman, whose light was within.'[17] The goddesses carved in the rock of the Dordogne and the Goddess of Willendorf are no maidens. Their hips swell; their full, rounded abdomens are a sign that their uteruses have held life; their breasts have been heavy with milk. At Catal Huyuk, in Anatolia, the Mother Goddess is represented as maiden, woman giving birth and grandmother. The Grandmother Goddesses of the Palaeolithic were replaced by the pregnant goddesses of the Neolithic. When new goddesses ascend in the pantheon older ones become Grandmother Goddesses, and they are often the most powerful of all. The Goddess Demeter, herself a Grandmother Goddess, developed out of the Mesopotamian goddess of fertility. Her effigies were made in corn, rye, maize or rice. Still today in some agricultural communities the last sheaf is formed into the shape of a woman, and called the Grandmother. English corn dollies stem from this practice.

The old Grandmother Goddess became an underground goddess, as she did in medieval Europe when she turned into a witch. The witch cult retained elements of Grandmother Goddess worship. The witch has many similarities to Artemis/Diana, the Moon Goddess and Huntress. She became Tana, the goddess of witches, who mated with Lucifer, her brother, and, in the Italian witch cult, gave birth to Araelia, the witch Messiah. In the ninth century the Council of Ancyra warned against 'those wicked women, reverting to Satan, and seduced by the illusions and phantoms of demons' who 'believe and profess that they ride at night with Diana on certain beasts, with an innumerable company of women, passing over immense distances, obeying her commands, as their mistress.)[18]

The Hebrews worshipped a male warrior god. But they had first to destroy the Grandmother Goddesses of the earth and the home who, co-existing as local goddesses, symbolized female power. As a patriarchal religion took over, these goddesses became despised and rejected, though still honoured in secret by women. Semitic, nomadic herders of goats and sheep invaded the agricultural societies of the great river valleys whose cultures worshipped the Goddess, and as a male-dominated mythology suppressed the Mother Goddess religion, she was turned into an ancient Grandmother Goddess. The people of Babylon worshipped the great grandmother goddess Tiamat, the female power that was the energy behind all created things. The male gods gathered together to struggle against her. They had heard that the Grandma was coming. When she opened her mouth, the young god Marduk of Babylon sent winds into her throat that blew her to pieces, and then dismembered her and fashioned the earth and heavens out of her body.'

Australian Aboriginals in Arnhem Land and part of the Northern Territory worship the Grandmother Goddess in the Kunapipi cult, the cult of the 'Old Woman'. In fact, there are two of these grandmothers, sisters called the Wanwaluk, who wandered the earth in the primordial Dream Time. The Kunapipi is a post-puberty ritual, an initiation which follows on that of a boy into manhood. It is concerned with the spiritual maturation of a group of young men, as well as with the ritual rebirth of the primal energy which is expressed in fertility and the regeneration of the cosmos. Novices enter a triangular sacred dancing place, symbolically re-entering the womb of the Grandmother Goddess, and emerge regenerated. The drama is enacted not just for the young men but for society as a whole, and not only for human beings but for all living things. The Grandmother Goddess replenishes the earth.

The Eager-to-be
Grandmother

In our northern industrial culture grandmothers are no longer icons. To become a grandmother does not represent for most of us a pinnacle of achievement in our lives. Certainly no one is going to worship us, or see us as the precious link between human beings and the ancestral gods. Nor are we given *carte blanche* to behave any way we like or to negotiate all family matters as grandmothers do in Taiwan. It is impossible for any modern grandmother to live up to the image of a goddess and women who look forward to being grandmothers do not expect to be treated like goddesses. Despite this, many women *ache* to be grandmothers. It is not just that they look forward to it in a vague, general way. For them it is a treat in store. A woman who feels like this sometimes has romantic ideas about how cosy and loving family life is going to be once the baby has arrived, and about her central place in the family nest. For her, becoming a grandmother holds promise of a life that is more fulfilled and meaningful – that will bring more love, and show that she is *needed*.

There are women who cannot wait to be grandmothers. If their children do not produce grandchildren they take it as a personal failing. Their yearning to have a grandchild is as strong as the yearning to have a child may be for a woman who cannot get pregnant. They anticipate babies long before a son or daughter feels ready for them or is certain that they have found the right partner. They eye every friend and casual acquaintance to whom they are introduced in terms of his or her potential as a parent to their grandchild. They start collecting playthings, picture books, baby clothes, 'just in case'. They often assume that sons and daughters are heterosexual and want a 'normal family'. A hidden anxiety that their children may be homosexual drives them to put a son or daughter under pressure to demonstrate that they are, after all, 'normal'. Perhaps a couple start living together and the eager-to-be grandmother asks her daughter questions like,

'When are you going to settle down?' If the daughter does not have a male partner the mother offers detailed descriptions of how happy girls with whom she went to school and daughters of friends and neighbours are, now that they have husbands and families.

Both married and unmarried daughters and daughters-in-law often feel intensely irritated by the older woman's expectations. This introduces great stresses in a relationship – especially with a woman who is already in her thirties and may be totally involved with and happy in her career, with one who has come to the decision that she does not want to bring babies into a violent and polluted world, a lesbian daughter who has no plans to start a family, or one who cannot conceive.

It is easy to forget that many couples are childless involuntarily – at least five million of them in the USA[1]. We can never know the exact number because infertility is shrouded in secrecy and a couple often do not want to talk about it and may never seek treatment. A stigma is attached to infertility, and a woman who cannot get pregnant struggles not to have to tell her mother, and especially her mother-in-law, that she has a problem. If she feels ashamed about it she may try to keep it a secret from everybody. It is like a curse – sometimes for having terminated a previous unwanted pregnancy. For a man it may feel like an attack on his masculinity. Elizabeth's mother accused her of being selfish and 'obsessed' with her academic career because she 'wouldn't have babies for Richard'. In fact, Elizabeth desperately wanted a baby, but her husband was sterile. She had a range of tests before he agreed to be tested and it was discovered that he had no viable sperm. She started to plan *in vitro* fertilisation with donor sperm, but he was adamant that he would never consider the baby his child.

Whether or not a couple hope for a baby, when a grandmother expresses her eagerness to have a grandchild, she risks intruding on the intimacy of their relationship, '*when* you have children' – not '*if* you have children'. It puts a daughter or daughter-in-law under pressure to get pregnant not because she and her partner want it to happen, but because of the older woman's striving to be a 'complete' family, her longing to be reassured that the future will not be empty, or simply her wish to establish that everything is 'normal', and that she, like her friends, has grandchildren of whom she can be proud and whose lives she can share. A woman may also see becoming a grandmother as part of her personal 'development'. A 64-year-old psychiatrist, writing a diary about becoming a grandmother said, 'I feel too old to be a grandmother for the first time. One tends to think of children contributing to one's growth but I imagine that mine have *held up my development*.'[2] Four months later on in her daughter's pregnancy the same expectant grandmother said that she felt too *young* to be a grandmother and that as a professional woman she found it threatening to be thought of primarily as a grandmother, 'The idea is so overwhelming I can't get it all together. I will have to rework every important aspect of my present life as well as the past . . . to become whole again on this new level.'[3]

Many women feel they are expected to have a baby or to produce a second child because over-eager grandmothers have planned it that way, and believe that any woman who does not want to be a mother, or who does not enjoy motherhood, is self-centred or is putting her career first in a manner 'unnatural' for a woman. An older woman may even see the absence of a pregnancy as an act of personal hostility and cruel rejection on her daughter's part. It is as if she is exploiting her independence – proclaiming that she is self-sufficient – and what is interpreted as her aggressive refusal to be a mother is a weapon that is used against her.

To become a grandmother provides confirmation of a woman's own identity, an assurance of its existence, to be revealed in the personality traits, aptitudes and values of her grandchildren. She looks to grandchildren for life's continuity. Once they are born she searches their faces, watches their behaviour, looks for every sign of this continuity.

It can be less egocentric than it appears, for these women who yearn to be grandmothers see their own lives as part of a family history, and this strong sense of belonging to a family with a heritage is part of their longing for grandchildren. Men sometimes feel it as strongly as women, for in a patrilineal society it is their lineage which will be assured and strengthened by the birth of a grandchild – and especially a grandson.

Many families have experienced hardship, poverty and discrimination – hounded from one country to another in great waves of nationalism and ethnic and religious persecution.

Some have survived systematic mass genocide. Brave individuals resisted oppression, struck out for new lands, and once there established homesteads and built careers. The birth of grandchildren can be an affirmation that their own grandparents' and great-grandparents' lives were worth while – that their struggles were not wasted. It is, in a way, a victory over injustice – a triumph over the Holocaust. A Jewish woman describes how she took her newborn twins to her mother's house and told her she had given them the Hebrew names of her own dead grandparents. Her mother said, 'I have got my mother and father back.'[4]

The significance of this inner meaning that the birth of a grandchild carries is often not understood by those who are becoming parents. They may brush it aside as irrelevant, part of a history which they do not want to share. The emotions that you express may seem to them sentimental and embarrassing. It may even appear that you are trying to take a personal experience from them and make it your own.

Grandparents with a strong sense of lineage can put intolerable pressure upon their children to reproduce. A woman who cannot conceive says, 'My mother-in-law has been pushing for a grandchild since the day we got married.' Her brother and sister both have children, but her husband is the senior son, so the parents attach vital importance to him producing a family.[5]

It is strange that in a modern society where we do not need children who will grow up to till the fields, to shepherd the flocks, to feed us in old age, where most of us do not own land, camels or great houses that we want to pass on to our heirs, we still think it important that our children have children. We may try to justify this by saying that we want a daughter to be 'fulfilled as a woman' and know the joy of motherhood, though experience must have shown us that motherhood is a whole lot more than joy and fulfilment. It brings inevitable suffering, and can erode a woman's identity while she is trying her hardest to be a good mother. A woman should have the opportunity of leading a full and satisfying life without becoming a mother, in the same way that a man can be successful and happy without becoming a father. There are many roads to fulfilment besides the biological.

If a woman's life has fallen to pieces through separation or divorce, illness, being made redundant, or through the death of a partner, it is tempting to believe that the birth of a grandchild will make everything right again and give hope for the future. Some women who are isolated and alone, and who do not have satisfying work to do, use their grandchildren to comfort them and to fill the loneliness. A 42-year-old grandmother had to give up the job she loved as a singer in tourist hotels. With the loss of her job came loss of self-esteem. She has taken her three small grandchildren under her wing and says, 'I'd go bananas at home if I didn't have my grandchildren to talk to.' She is putting her life on hold, and avoiding the question of what else she is going to do, because her grandchildren need her. But this is only a temporary solution. The children will grow up and grow away.

For some women becoming a grandmother represents a second chance. It promises an opportunity to mother in ways in which they believe they failed with their own children. As one woman put it, 'I was so busy when my children were young that I missed having any relationship with them. Now I can make up for that with my grandchildren.' This is a worthy sentiment, but if it is the only reason why she is enthusiastic about being a grandmother it entails using the children to satisfy her own needs, to fill a void in her life, to attempt to absolve the guilt that comes with her sense of failure as a mother. It does not auger well for her relationship with her sons and daughters, who may feel bitter and resentful as they watch the woman who never seemed to have time for them when they were children now putting on the successful 'granny act'.

So if your daughter or daughter-in-law has not made you a grandmother, and you are eager for her to, it is wise to pull back, leave her space, and avoid intruding on her privacy with your doubts and anxieties. Drop your shoulders and relax! Be there for her if she wants to discuss the subject, and listen, rather than saying what you think and offering advice.

Why didn't she tell me she was pregnant?

Any woman who is in emotional overload about having grandchildren is unlikely to hear about a pregnancy until it is several months on the way. This is not because a daughter is hostile. It is a protective device. For many women in early pregnancy there is a storm of emotions to be weathered – and sometimes for their partners, too. However much they wanted to get pregnant, the reality comes as a shock. If the pregnancy is an accident there are decisions to be made, doubts to be confronted – perhaps also negotiations that take place – and a way found to accept the pregnancy. Whether or not they experience these mixed emotions, a couple may treasure the intimate time in which they alone know or suspect that conception has occurred. A shared secret bonds them in a way that secret information bonds all conspirators. To tell their mothers – especially if they are likely to be emotionally over-involved on the subject of babies – is to risk intruding on and destroying that precious intimacy. If a woman has had previous miscarriages, or she thinks that she might not be able to hold onto the pregnancy because she is having intermittent bleeding, or she has decided to have tests for genetic disabilities, and has to wait for the results before she tells anyone about being pregnant, there is even more reason why she may not wish to involve her mother – and especially her mother-in-law – until much later. It is important for a grandmother to understand this, and be willing to stand back and be happy to be told about the coming baby at a time which feels right to the pregnant woman herself.

Some women remember the time when they had babies as the high point of their lives. It may be because they now feel lonely and unwanted. If you have little purpose in your life except getting through the housework each day, trivia assume increased importance, and memories of a time when you were active and needed are sweeter. The romanticization of motherhood is, in such circumstances, the result of selective recollection – clinging to rosy pictures and forgetting the bad ones. But it would be wrong to blame individual women for the tendency to do this. For it is the consequence of a social system in which men weald power and women do the menial tasks. Women who were never trained to have careers or to cope with life outside the home with any competence have often looked to, and found, fulfilment in domestic life, and for them caring for babies has been empowering. When all the children have left home, and especially when a husband has died, a woman who has found these things satisfying may be left with an aching void and a longing to love and care for a child who is dependent on her and needs her.

On the other hand, it is unlikely that any woman has experienced fulfilment and maintained her confidence through all the stages of her mothering. For mothering is a complex skill, and we do not have equal self-assurance or pleasure through all its different stages. Some women enjoy babies, but not two year olds. Some like their eight to ten year olds more than either their babies or their adolescents. The feeling of being in control often disappears entirely by the time children are in their teens. Grandmothers have been through all that and may welcome having babies again because they think they have the skills, know what *ought* to happen, and can lay down ground rules of child-rearing from their own practical experience of mothering.

This is dangerous territory. In any culture in which traditions and child-rearing customs have been fractured, as they have throughout North America and most of Europe, each woman has to learn how to mother in her own way and in her own time, and any skills that can be handed down and advice given are likely to be discredited. Most grandmothers are aware of this and are careful to avoid giving advice – sometimes even when it would be welcome! As one woman told me when her first grandchild was born, 'I decided never to give advice – even if I was asked to.'

A woman who has devoted herself to caring for her family often finds, once the children have left home, that her husband relies more and more on the steady servicing he has taken for granted through the years when children were at home. Perhaps he dies, and her whole *raison d'être* has disappeared. Many women have the courage to make new lives for themselves then. Others, lacking educational skills and self-confidence, often feel socially isolated and sometimes depressed, and are unable to do this. The birth of grandchildren offers them fresh hope, and they long to be fully involved. But it is not what their daughters and daughters-in-law want.

As the birth approaches, questions to the pregnant woman about whether anything has happened yet, how she feels, and if there are signs that labour might be starting, bring guarded, even evasive, responses. She may feel under attack – as if her mother is trying to take over the birth experience. This is her body, not a replay of her mother's birth experience, and she does not want the older woman to stage-manage it. The baby is *her* baby, not part of a dynasty.

There is another problem, too. Emotions are infectious. A grandmother who had a bad experience of birth herself, and who is afraid that something might go wrong, may intrude her own emotions on the pregnancy and birth in a way that can be damaging. Her sympathy may be overwhelming so that, to protect herself, the younger woman pushes it aside impatiently, or the grandmother may seem more concerned about the safety of the baby than the mother's happiness and well-being. This makes her daughter or daughter-in-law feel as if she is merely an incubator for the precious baby.

Equally, a grandmother who enjoyed birth and babies, or who only remembers the good parts, and so in retrospect tends to romanticize them, imposes on the younger woman in another way. She does not leave her space for her own experience – for acknowledging and facing up to real feelings, which may well include doubt, apprehension, fear, even anger, and which can be very intense. When you unravel memory it is vital to see the colours of the whole pattern of experience. To do anything else is dishonest. You do not have to narrate your own story, to describe each detail of how it was for you. Stand back, leave space. Be there when you are needed.

A grandmother who is on hand can give support, serve as a resource when needed, offer encouragement and help build a new mother's self-esteem. But she is not an authority on child-rearing, however many children she has had herself. She may be as much at sea about baby care as the new mother herself. Even when it comes to simple actions like whether you put a baby down to sleep on her side, her back or her front, whether or not you wedge her with a rolled blanket or pillow, whether the window in the room at night should be open or closed, and whether the baby should sleep in another room, in the mother's bed or in a cot close to her, professional counsel and fashions in child care are changing rapidly. And when it comes to the crunch no one, except the mother herself, can be certain what is right for a baby, for babies have personalities and express their wishes in no uncertain ways. Every mother – and every grandmother, too – needs above all to learn from the baby.

The grandmother sisterhood

When you become a grandmother you start meeting other women who have grandchildren of about the same age and who want to compare experiences and talk about their wonderful grandchildren. Often you become aware that women, whom you knew before, are grandmothers, but you never thought of them in that role, and a new area of conversation opens up. Listening to granny talk, it is obvious that there is competition, sharing of hopes, plans and progress, and some commiseration. Women with grandchildren discover that there is a new sisterhood out there. They are one of a club. As one woman put it, 'We're a gaggle of friends who are all completely in love with being grandmothers. It's fun! We are even thinking of going off for weekends together.'

In fact, sometimes one reason why a woman longs to be a grandmother is that she is shut out from membership of this granny sisterhood. She feels that she has *failed* to produce a grandchild and is missing out on a stage of life which is a reward for having children. It is one element in the hopes of over-eager grandmothers who feel that unless they are presented with a grandchild they are being denied the reward of all their hard work as mothers. When other women ask them, 'How many grandchildren do you have?' they are ashamed when they have to say, 'None . . . yet.'

It is often assumed that every woman in her fifties or sixties has grandchildren as part of the normal course of events. Not to be a grandmother seems like a deprivation, something which a woman has to excuse and explain away to friends of the same age. It is not only that most couples are under pressure to have children, but that older women are put under social pressure to become grandmothers, too. So we may make the mistake of asking, tentatively at first, 'When are you planning to have children? . . . Do you want a baby? . . . Is anything wrong? . . . Have you been to the doctor? . . . Don't you think you ought to find out? . . . Are you *trying*?' The questioning, the hints, can be insistent. Sometimes it is as if the daughters and daughters-in-law are entered into a competion to discover who can have babies first and how fast they can reproduce. One who cannot put a baby in the grandmother's arms is a failure.

The designer grandchild

A grandmother sometimes makes blatant use of her grand-children for self-enhancement. Meetings become mere photo opportunites, which take the place of any real relationship. It is as if the baby is a family or personal possession which granny wants to show off to her friends. The grandchild is dressed up, exhibited and displayed as a superbaby in appearance, motor or intellectual development, or good behaviour. This is stressful and irritating for the child's mother, and may be one reason why she does not enjoy visits to granny and defers them whenever she can. For any grandmother who adores her grandchild it is tempting to show people how clever or pretty she is. There is nothing intrinsically wrong with this, except when it results in the child being used as a style accessory, in the same way that babies are used in advertisements promoting toiletries and perfumes, or are depicted in the arms of glamorous models on the covers of glossy magazines.

Hello published a piece about Gina Lollobrigida in 'the latest role which has come her way, that of being a grandmother to Dimitri Milko Skofic'. There are photographs of the star in three costume changes, posing in the garden with her four-month-old grandson. The copy says, 'Full of pride, she wanted to present him in the grandiose style she has grown accustomed to, and invited the cameras into the garden of her magnificent home in Appia Antica, Rome.'[6]

A woman says of her mother-in-law, 'When she comes it is only to take photographs. She doesn't do anything to help. I can be working myself into the ground and she is there with her camera. She wants snaps to show her friends.' The presents she gives, the frilly knickers, the pretty dresses, the bib with 'Baby' embroidered on it, are all intended to enhance this image of a perfect baby and granny. Girls run the risk of being put on display to exhibit their femininity. A grandmother may enjoy buying fancy dresses and curling a child's hair. A pretty granddaughter is treasured and exhibited like an ornament.

Sometimes it goes further than that. The child beauty pageant scene offers challenge, excitement and the thrill of competition to some American grandmothers – particularly in southern states. Little girls are trained from as young as four months, and grandmothers help to pay the huge costs of plane fares, entering the pageant (up to $1000), modelling, dance, singing and voice production courses, elaborate dresses that may cost as much as $700, hair styles, salon and beauty treatments, and hotel bills and food. These pageants unite mothers and daughters and bring glamour in their efforts to inject excitement into otherwise humdrum lives. There is the ten month old who has been in close on twenty competitions already. 'Pageants are something we do together,' her mother says, and the grandmother explains that it is 'a way of spending time with the children. It's a bonding thing.' She justifies the pressure that she puts on her granddaughter by saying, 'She's happy with herself. That's what these pageants make you.'[7] Grandmothers often get together in the pageant business. Bunny is a hairdresser and styles her three-year-old granddaughter's hair, while Shirley, her other grandmother, constructs the costumes, 'It brings us together . . . We always take along Velcro, glue, needles and thread, extra sequins and rosebuds to the event. It's like travelling with a show and she's the star. Our job is to keep her happy.'

A designer grandchild may play along with her assigned role because she is rewarded by attention and love. As she gets older, however, she often fails to conform. She refuses to play the piano in front of her grandmother's friends, or demonstrate how well-behaved she is, and resists listing her exam successes. Then grandmother and grandchild are set on a collision course, and visits with granny are tasks to be endured, or – worse still – ordeals which the child has to be bribed to undergo.

It may be not so much a matter of exhibiting a particular child as having to put on a performance as a harmonious family. Some grandmothers are interested mainly in demonstrating family 'togetherness'. They long to show that they have a united family in which everyone loves everyone else. In any family it is highly improbable that this is an accurate representation of relationships at all times – even when there is genuine affection. It puts families under strain and, especially as grandchildren become teenagers, means that they feel they cannot be their 'real' selves when the family is gathered to please granny. No wonder they sometimes opt out of these family occasions!

There are so many mistakes an exultant grandmother can make that it is not surprising that some women feel bewildered. They adore their grandchildren and are trying to do their best. Why isn't it working out? Is there a key to how to be a grandmother who is supportive but not interfering, there to help without criticizing, strong but not overbearing, interested in the children but not forcing them to put on an act, loving but not over-indulgent? Perhaps that key is to recognize each child as a unique individual, to respect the child's personality from birth onwards, and to stand back and enjoy grandchildren at each stage of growth without trying to force the pace or mould them. Maybe that is the essence of a mutual relationship of love and trust with our children who are parents and with our grandchildren.

The Reluctant
Grandmother

B eing told that you are to be a grandmother brings a sudden sea change. In a matter of seconds the tide of your life turns. Many women are overjoyed; many others are torn by conflicting emotions.

It is hard to admit this, because everyone expects you to be happy. But for many women being a fully involved grandmother spells extra responsibilities at a period in their lives when for the first time they can choose from a variety of options. That is why you may see it as losing your freedom. Yet it may not be these new commitments that make a woman anxious but that her self-image is being forced to change. It can be difficult for anyone who has not been through the experience to understand this. The new role seems like a misfit, as if you were handed a stranger's clothes to wear, 'I don't *feel* like a granny!' You are not the only woman who protests, 'But I'm not ready to be a grandmother yet!'

The news that you are to be a grandmother is often a bigger milestone on the road to realizing that you are ageing than the menopause. After all, the menopause is simply the cessation of menstrual periods. For most women that is a relief: no more tampons, no more menstrual cramps and backache, no more mess. And for those who disliked monthly mood swings and other conditions linked with the menstrual cycle it is a liberation from pre-menstrual tension, migraine, and other hormone-related illnesses. Only around ten per cent of women confront problems with the menopause, though the manufacturers of hormone replacement therapy make a big deal of hot flushes, emotional agitation and the risks of osteoporosis. Becoming a grandmother brings with it for some women a sense of being 'over the hill'. As one woman put it, 'Life was passing me by. It meant no more babies for me. I felt cheated.' The crisis point was not the knowledge that her biological clock told her that she was no longer fertile, which she had taken in her stride, but learning that her daughter was pregnant. She suddenly felt replaced.

Going through the menopause and becoming a grandmother for the first time often coincide. For many women, becoming a grandmother around the time of menopause is a positive experience. It brings a sense of the flow of women's lives, as a woman ceases menstruating while her daughter gives birth to a baby. 'The beauty of the timing,' a woman writes as she waits for the news that her grandchild is born, 'is that my daughter is having this miracle of life as I am menopausal.' She sees it as 'a time of passages as this soul comes to life, as Sindy moves into her parenting role, and I pass into another phase of my life.'

Much that has been researched and written about women's emotional reactions to the menopause may, in fact, be associated with becoming a grandmother. Understanding of the significance of this transition has been obscured by the emphasis put on the menopause as the single important life event in a woman's middle age, and by treating it as a medical condition rather than a life passage. It is easier to explain mid-life crisis and the stresses of the years between 40 and 55 – the feeling that some women have of being trapped and 'used' or 'drained' and useless – in terms of biology, than by acknowledging the social pressures and the switch in self-image and public image that come with being identified as a grandmother.

Memories of our own grandmothers are unlikely to offer any magic key to how *we* should be. The world has changed and we have different goals in life. We are far too busy with careers and other commitments to act the part of the comfortable, grey-haired 'grandma in the kitchen' with a soft lap and endless time to tell stories.

In traditional cultures, as we have seen, becoming a grandmother brings enhanced status. You have reared children, married daughters and found good wives for your sons, and now you are rewarded for the long struggle of being a mother. Your own life, and the lives of your parents and grandparents, are extended into the future. As one Greek peasant grandmother put it, 'I live as far as little Christos', her baby grandson.[1] Your self-image is enriched, and other people perceive you as having increased status. Your garden is fruitful.

In Western cultures, in contrast, a woman often feels discarded. Over and over again grandmothers tell me, 'I try not to interfere. I am careful never to voice my opinion. I realize that my ideas must be out of date.' For we have been brainwashed by experts. Paediatricians, GPs, nurses, health visitors may warn a new mother not to listen to her mother and listen to experts like them instead. Mother-in-law and granny jokes, and the ways in which older women are represented in TV sit-coms, reflect the suspicion, fear and often sheer hatred associated with ageing women. There are positive, idealized images too, of course. In TV series of romantic rural life (the prototype was *The Waltons*), grannies are nurturers, giving selflessly of their wisdom, love and ancient skills, and their knowledge of traditional remedies for every ill. They are generous, warm providers. Children and grandchildren come to them with their problems. They are on hand with home-baked cakes and pies, ready sympathy and solutions to every difficulty.

But positive images of the grandmother role can be threatening, too, because they impose an ideal. The point about any ideal is that it is impossible to attain. It is a dream, a distant goal, a chimera. A woman who tries to live up to the ideal grandmother image is bound to fail. She is also at risk of having her life disrupted when at last it has become organized after years of coping with chaos, being at everyone's beck and call, as she brought up her children. When they left home there was a precious hard-won, new-found freedom and finally she felt able to do what *she* wanted and to develop skills and interests it was impossible to do while she was younger. But that blessed feeling of release may not last long. Adult children today belong to the boomerang generation: they go off to college, train for jobs, may be unable to get them, and economic pressure often forces them back to dependency, by this time with babies. Some grandmothers revel in this. For others it is an intrusion on precious personal space. It is a taboo subject, but when grandmothers talk honestly about their feelings that word 'cheated' often crops up, 'I don't want to lose my freedom when I have only just achieved it. I feel cheated.'

Some women had high hopes for their daughters and are concerned that a young woman is thoughtlessly giving up her freedom and career opportunities – and the right to be herself, not only a wife and mother. A grandmother told me that she was horrified to hear of her daughter's pregnancy, exclaiming, 'Why do women feel they have to do this – sacrificing their independence?' Anyone who has felt trapped by marriage and babies, on a treadmill of domesticity and child-rearing, may struggle to enable a daughter to make for herself a different kind of life, and be very disappointed when she seems to be repeating her mother's mistakes. Any woman who has fought hard for an education, to make a career for herself, to climb the ladder of success, may also feel that her daughter is opting out and missing everything that makes life zing. They may be wrong, but this is how these grandmothers feel, and their daughters pick up on such attitudes with unfailing accuracy.

There may be practical reasons, too, why a woman is aghast at the news that she is about to become a grandmother. If you first had children when you were in your twenties, and then again in your late thirties or forties, perhaps with a different partner, as many women do nowadays, your younger ones may still be a more or less full-time responsibility because they are pre-teens or even pre-school. A woman whose youngest child was eight and had also provided day care for children for twenty years, explained, 'For the last twenty-four years I have had at least one child under five years old in the house.' She could not believe the degree to which her life changed for the better as soon as she stopped caring for little ones. It is not surprising that when she learned that an older daughter was about to make her a grandmother she felt that her life had been hijacked and protested, 'But I'm not ready to *give* to another baby!'

In her prime

For every woman who mourns her empty nest and wonders what on earth she is going to do with the rest of her life when the young leave home, there are many others for whom the post-child years hold new opportunities, challenges and excitement. The focus of activity shifts outside the home. This may baffle your children, who are rather alarmed at this new granny dynamo who has to consult her diary before she can commit herself to family engagements. As one daughter puts it, 'Gran is happy to look after the boys, and says how much she likes to see them, but in practice this is not so straightforward, because she and Grandpa spend so much of their time doing courses, going on club outings, reading for the blind, and going to the theatre and opera. Retirement is a full-time job for them! It gets quite hard finding a place to slot into their schedule.'

'One's prime is elusive,' Miss Jean Brodie advised her pupils. 'You little girls, when you grow up, must be on the alert to recognise your prime at whatever time of your life it may occur. You must then live it to the full.'[2] A woman in middle age often discovers that she is in her prime. If she has the courage to live it to the full it can be disconcerting for her family.

Monica has six children, now all grown up, and a large brood of grandchildren. She flung herself into motherhood – she had no choice about it – and devoted her life to her husband and children. She could not wait for them to marry, settle down and give her grandchildren, and she and her husband Charles presided over huge weddings to which friends and family travelled from many countries. It looked as if she was born to be a grandmother – and would adore it. But in her mid-fifties, after an illness which made her think about herself and what *she* wanted, she found herself getting increasingly irritated with the grandchildren, who always seemed to be underfoot, and whom she considered quite undisciplined.

One wet winter Monica gave her husband a hand with making a stained-glass lampshade from a kit. It turned out well and he thought he would make something else. Monica was talking with the vicar of the local church and discovered that he wanted a stained-glass window to replace the plain one over the altar, but there was not much money available. 'My husband makes stained glass. He'll do it,' she promised. Charles was appalled, but there was no turning back now. They started finding out more about stained glass, began to design a window, went to the Czech Republic to get special vivid blue dyes, and piece by piece, pane by pane, they made their stained-glass window. It was a great success, and they were asked to do a restaurant window, then another church window, and it is now a shared enterprise which is absorbing more and more of their lives. Monica has reached the point where she does not want to have the grandchildren to stay.

'You can use the house, but I shan't be there,' she says, and though she is happy to meet them at big family gatherings, she has cut loose. Elizabeth, her oldest daughter, says, 'She is really a very bad grandmother!' Monica is in her prime. And she does not intend to waste it.

For more and more women, being able to move on from the long phase of their lives when they were bearing children presents an opportunity to do something other than feeding hungry mouths, clearing up messes and trying to make order out of chaos. But for many there are obstacles. From the mid-forties until the late fifties they are often trapped into being carers of the young, the old, and often the very young. In fact, women nowadays spend longer caring for the elderly than they do for their children.[3] No wonder that in many different societies mid-life women talk about suffering from 'nerves'. It is not because they are menopausal, but because of the enormous pressures on them as nurturers.

Women often become assertive for the first time in their lives when they reach the age of forty plus. Some go further than this and become angry. All the pent-up frustrations of endless housework, child-rearing and the servicing of men at last emerge. There may be little they can do to change these conditions, but at least they can express it in an accepted cultural idiom as 'nerves' because of the menopause. An anthropologist found that 80 per cent of menopausal women whom she studied in Peru said they suffered from 'nervios'.[4] They yelled at the children, lost their tempers and criticized everything and everyone. Their 'nervios' allowed them to express the anger they felt, and everyone agreed that the cure was to get out of the home, visit friends, go to the cinema and be relieved of their usual responsibilities to men. The menopause enabled them to achieve all this! For women with little education and very restricted lives it was liberating.

In many countries there have been enormous social changes over the last twenty or thirty years that have changed the role of the grandmother. They have occurred in rural as well as in urban areas, and in regions where there remains strong traditions.

Catherine's husband died after a long, debilitating illness through which she devoted herself to his care. They lived in a small French village where the men divided their time between fishing and working their vineyards, and the women did housework, cooked, and met at the *boulangerie* each morning to buy *flûtes* straight from the oven, and the *lavoir* the open-air public laundry, where they shared news and found emotional support and practical help from each other. Women shared chores with their daughters and daughters-in-law and families spilled over between houses, so that a grandson, uncle or cousin, or cousin twice removed, might have a bedroom in any relative's home. The result was that houses were honeycombed with members of extended kin groups. But the village became depopulated as young people left to find work in the cities. The introduction of domestic technology, including washing machines, and the arrival of a supermarket down the road, led to the closing down of the *lavoir* and the *boulangerie*, and ultimately the disintegration of this women-to-women network. Catherine was lonely and her life became very restricted.

After her husband's death she kicked over the traces, entered a relationship with a man who lived in the town nearby, discarded her sprigged cotton frocks and aprons for a chic new dress style, wore make-up for the first time, had her hair cut and permed, and moved out from her home. Her only son is a mason in the village, where he still lives with his wife and three children. When Catherine still lived in the village she often had her grandchildren for an hour or two, and showed them off proudly. Now she has her son's children to stay with her under duress for two or three days each summer. She says she is worn out with cooking meals and caring for these lively youngsters (who seemed impeccably well-behaved to me). That switch in life-style has taken place within the last ten years.

Traditionally in this part of Languedoc grandmothers are deeply involved in the lives of their children and grand-children. Marriages are made within the village. When the carpenter's son married, his father was concerned that it was not a local girl. In fact, she lived in the next village, all of five kilometres away. Catherine's son's wife comes from near Paris, so Catherine cannot chat and share respon-sibilities with the other grandmother. The family is frag-mented.

Baby-minding

In spite of these profound social changes grandmothers are expected to be accessible, to baby-sit, to take over child care while a daughter goes to work or on holiday, to assist financially – and to *enjoy* it. One grandmother says, 'I hate being taken for granted. But they just say "Grandma loves doing it"!' If you are on hand, you may slip into a role which, in your absence, is that of the social services. Governments, too, often take it for granted that grandmothers are available for child care, and assume that relationships of support within families will fill gaps in social policies. Certainly in Britain and the United States of America there is no policy to support working parents, and an implicit assumption that female relatives will help out because this is what women do 'naturally', and what they must enjoy doing.

It is understandable that when a woman has worked her way through motherhood and entered on a stage of her life in which she has a career or is training for a new one, and is using the management skills she acquired as a mother, she is likely to be torn by conflicting emotions about becoming a grandmother. A woman who returned to college, started writing a newspaper column, and became 'enthralled with volley-ball' says her life was full, 'The emptying nest never looked so good.' So she felt ambivalent when told that she was about to become a grandmother. Another said, 'I have been through all that – having babies, bringing them up. I've done my bit. If she wants children she ought to look after them. I don't think it's right for me to have them while she is gallivanting around. When she's at work, that's different – because I know they need the money.' A woman who feels the same way, that she does not want to be 'used' explained, 'I don't believe in looking after the children while she is out working. I love having them here when we make proper arrangements, for a weekend for instance, and I baby-sit at her house while she goes to the leisure centre every Thursday evening. But I don't want to be tied down. I retired early to get freedom, not to be a baby-minder.' Another grandmother, recently retired from a career in management, complains, 'They take it for granted that I'll look after the grandchildren in the school holidays, but they never even take me out for a meal.' When I asked her why she had not told her daughter how she felt she said she dare not 'rock the boat'. A mother of a single mother with a fifteen month old says, 'I am never free to look after myself.' She describes herself as 'wife, mother, nurse, agony aunt, cook, shopper, cleaner, doormat, listener, counsellor, daughter' as well as full-time grandmother. She longs to ditch all these responsibilities and have some personal space for herself. But she feels guilty about it. 'After eighteen years of being at home with children and another eighteen years in a full-time career, I didn't want any structure, no weekly commitment. I wanted to feel free.' Most of all, women want freedom.

Many women in the past never encountered such problems because they slipped straight from being mothers to grand-mothers. The role of grandmother of the family grew, as if spontaneously and without any interval, from that of being a mother. They never experienced that mid-life heady taste of freedom.

A mother-in-law tends to be more out-spoken in her views about these things than the woman's own mother. As we shall see in chapter 12, mothers-in-law do not feel under the same obligation to help, and may be wary of doing so in case they put extra stresses on the relationship with a daughter-in-law, 'With my own daughter I can say what I think. But with my daughter-in-law I know I must stand back – not interfere. It's best to leave her to get on with it, even when I disagree. I don't offer to have the children because it would make things difficult between us.'

A woman is less likely to ask for help from her mother-in-law than her mother. This is partly because she does not feel entitled to it, except in an emergency. It is also partly because a maternal grandmother often has approximately the same values and attitudes to child-rearing as her daughter. If she does not, the two women can usually talk about their different viewpoints and negotiate what should happen (though it does not always work out like that in practice). But the younger woman may be very unsure about her mother-in-law's beliefs and practices. She often suspects that shortcomings in her male partner's behaviour can be put down to the way in which he was brought up, 'She neglected him. She adored his brother, but I think he was deprived. So he has never had any self-confidence', 'She fed him on extraordinary things. She didn't know anything about nutrition – and still doesn't. I couldn't possibly leave the kids with her for more than a couple of hours.'

Some daughters-in-law manage to be pragmatic about the differences, as was the one who said, 'There are times when we haven't got on, when I would have liked not to have been relying on her. And because you rely on somebody I think you have to compromise on values and behaviour and what you allow – and I have had to come to terms with that and it hasn't always been easy.'[5]

Teenage pregnancy

For many North American mothers their initiation into grand-motherhood is to be told by a teenage daughter that she is having a baby. The United States has the highest rate of teenage pregnancies in the Western world, estimated at one million each year. In Britain, in contrast, the rate of teenage pregnancies is fast decreasing and is one third lower than it was at the end of the 1960s.

It is a shock to be presented with a grandchild when you perceive your daughter as still only a child herself, especially if she has no partner. A woman said that when her seventeen year old told her she was pregnant she was 'overwhelmed as my youngest child was then only thirteen, and I felt I hadn't had a chance to finish being a mother and enjoy a child-free gap between. I felt resentment, too, that she only told me she was pregnant at five months, and we didn't even know she had a boyfriend.' To her mother's dismay, Nicola announced her engagement simultaneously with her pregnancy on her eighteenth birthday. Her mother says she and her boyfriend are permanently unemployed. He is a heavily tattooed ex-convict whom she had known for only a month.

Rachel was brought up in a Mennonite household where values were strict and extra-marital pregnancy considered very shocking. She told me that her cousin had to get up

in front of the whole church to confess her sin when she got
pregnant before marriage. Now in her late forties, the last ten
years with three teenagers have been horrendous for Rachel.
There have been violent clashes, mostly about drugs, sex and
trouble at school, and she and her husband were in a 'Tough
Love' programme. This is an American system of giving love
within a strong framework of discipline, negotiating a young
person's better behaviour on the basis of strict but limited
rules of what is unacceptable, and never wavering as to
the consequences of failure to conform. A bitter argument
between the seventeen-year-old daughter, Sophie, and her
father culminated in her threatening to leave home. He replied,
'Go!' She left and moved in with her boyfriend, a few months
younger than herself. Two months later she asked her mother if
she would go shopping with her, 'But can we just sit and talk a
little before we go?' Very quickly she said, 'I'm pregnant.' 'Oh!'
I said in a shocked, disappointed way. She burst into tears, 'I
thought you'd be happy!' 'So there you have it,' her mother
comments. 'I quickly began the adjustment process.'

Sophie was ill during the first five months of her pregnancy
and Rachel went through nine months not really believing
that there would be a live, healthy baby at the end. 'I was
afraid to get into it. I was prepared for a miscarriage or a
baby with problems.' In the last few weeks Sophie developed
pre-eclampsia, which led to more anxiety. Then the baby was
born – a perfect little girl. Rachel picked her up and immediately
fell in love with her. Over the next four weeks she spent every
night at Sophie's house, walking with, rocking, singing to and
cuddling the baby each evening so that the new parents could
rest. 'A warm, tiny being against me. I loved it. Talk about
bonding. Oh boy! That was bonding!' Describing the special
relationship with her granddaughter she says, 'It is so different
from having three little ones under four years of age, which is
how we had ours, and being able to enjoy just one baby was
bliss.' Another side-effect of this birth is a much improved
relationship with her daughter, 'We are friends now.'

Much the same happened with another woman who was
shocked when her teenage daughter got pregnant, 'I felt rage,
sorrow, resentment, aimed at my daughter . . . The birth wasn't
how it should have been. There was no husband to hold her
hand. It was me that helped and comforted her throughout a

long, slow labour. I held Billy in my arms when he was just five minutes old, and all the fear, anger and anxieties melted away, and I loved him.'

Even if your daughter is older you may be reluctant to be made a grandmother until she is married, or at least in a steady relationship, 'I was horrified. She was at university and I assumed that she would have an abortion.' But this woman supported her daughter in her decision to have the baby and finds that being a grandmother is much more fun than she ever thought possible. One woman describes how her daughter rang her long-distance and the first thing she said was, 'Do you want to be a grandmother?' 'I'd love it,' I said, 'but not yet!' 'Well, you're going to be. I'm pregnant.' She had left the man who was the father of the baby, and was not even in the same country by the time she realized she was pregnant. 'She was 28,' her mother says, 'but when that happens your daughter becomes 10 years old again.' This grandmother adjusted rapidly to the situation, and she and her husband welcomed their daughter home with open arms. There was no question of it because, she says simply, 'We love our children.' They adore their grandson, who is now two and a half, though child-care arrangements remain a constant worry.

Some grandparents are left literally holding the baby. When their daughter, whose lover had come to the conclusion that fatherhood entailed too much responsibility, was drifting around with a highly unsuitable crowd, she left her 18-month-old son with her parents. He is still there at seven. They have a 17-year-old at home as well who has always treated Michael like a much younger brother, alternately teasing and spoiling him.[6] These grandparents say that the lifestyle their daughter leads and the friends she keeps are so bizarre that they could not subject a child, let alone their beloved grandson, to such an existence. The grandfather says, 'My planned mid-forties reading of the English classics has been postponed in favour of such stirring stuff as Teenage Mutant Ninja Turtles and Power Rangers.' Though it is hard work, this little boy is the greatest source of happiness in their lives for the past five years. They have rediscovered the joy of having young children around and comment wryly that the real problems of parenthood start only when children grow up.

Many reluctant grandmothers say that everything changed

once the baby was there. Anxiety gave way to delight as they got to know the baby, and discovered the excitement, deep satisfaction, and – for some – a new sense of purpose that this brought to their lives. A woman whose husband had died, without any warning, from a heart attack, has started to surface from her grief, and dares to love again. One with breast cancer, treated by a radical mastectomy, who has learned that secondary cancers have been diagnosed, relishes each day she can still spend with her grandchildren, and looks to the future beyond her own pain. Realizing that her daughter will not trust her to be alone with the baby, an alcoholic at last faces up to her illness, joins a self-help group and conquers her dependancy. Another, bored with a constant round of lunches, shopping and entertaining for her husband, finds that she is needed for more important things, and develops a new self-confidence. A woman who was stuck in a long conflict with a rebellious daughter emerges from the warfare battle-scarred but now able to communicate with her again, and with shared enthusiasm for a beautiful, brilliant baby!

To become a grandmother is to grow. It is a door flung open. A parched well filling with water. A tree in flower.

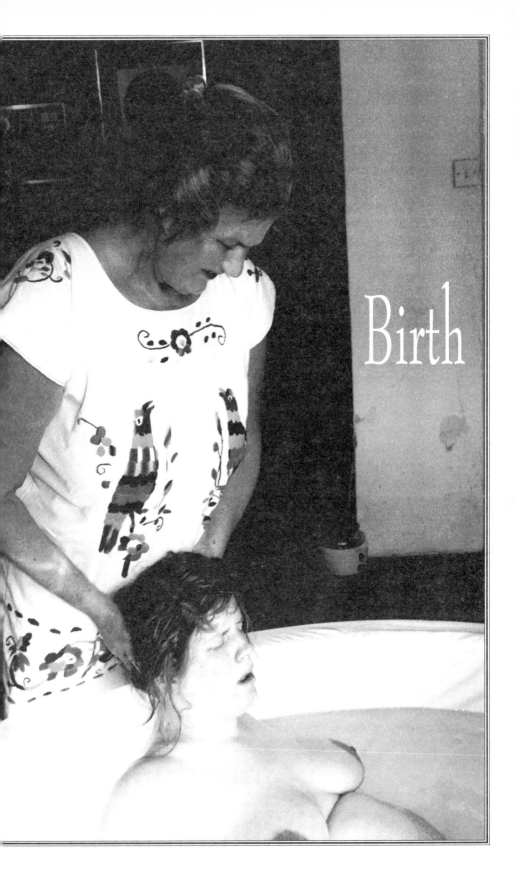

Birth

It is often difficult for a mother and daughter to communicate in a relaxed and spontaneous way because the management of pregnancy and birth has changed so much that there seems to be no bridge of experience between women of different generations. There are new screening procedures, a new technology of birth, and advice about weight gain, exercise in pregnancy and infant feeding, for example, which contradicts that which the older woman was given. This discontinuity of experience is a direct consequence of the appropriation of birth by the medical system. For the vast majority of women it is no longer a domestic process and the knowledge that is communicated within the family is very restricted.

Pregnancy

In traditional societies it is usually very different. Healing herbs used in pregnancy and birth and during lactation, advice about what food to eat and what to avoid, about the kinds of physical work and exercise it is good to do and those which should not be done, about sex, stress and personal relationships, and other emotional aspects of pregnancy, birth and motherhood, along with preparation for birth and breast-feeding, are passed down from grandmothers through mothers to daughters.

A Mexican mother-in-law, for example, becomes very close to her son's wife during pregnancy, advises her to walk a lot to keep her body lithe and her muscles strong, and never to go out if there is a lunar eclipse or else the baby may be born with a cleft palate. As one grandmother explains, 'These are our ancestor beliefs, who ruled their lives according to the moon.'[1] It is all part of the culture of women which still holds strong in many rural areas of predominantly traditional societies, but has been eroded in the cities and is laughed at as a load of 'old wives' tales'.

In industrial cultures grandmothers today are more likely to hand down 'old doctors' tales' – pronouncements about weight gain in pregnancy (if you put on a lot of weight you need a Caesarean section, for instance), the risk of birth difficulties if the mother's feet are small, risks of giving birth if you are over thirty-five, and rules that you have to be induced if you go a week 'overdue', and about the benefits of enemas, episiotomies, and electronic foetal monitoring, as well as feeding myths, having to use nipple shields if your nipples are flat or retracted, 'and you must breastfeed ten minutes each side every four hours', for example. These ideas were fashionable when they had their babies, but research has now discredited them.

We are beginning to realize that women's experiences – and the knowledge that has always been shared between women – is of value. While some grandmothers are being careful not to say what they and their mothers and grandmothers did, in case it is out of date, other women are trying to find out traditional birth and healing practices, about non-medical ways of coping with the discomforts of pregnancy and preparing for birth, and the healing herbs that women used to know, such as raspberry leaves and comfrey. When research is initiated into the properties of traditional herbal remedies it is often found that folk medicine has positive value in, for example, treating morning sickness, boosting a pregnant woman's haemoglobin level, and encouraging the flexibility of perineal tissues. I remember that my mother made large jugs of 'spring medicine' as a tonic every year, and also recommended this in pregnancy. It consisted of fresh young nettles and a large bunch of parsley boiled in water and strained with home-made barley water, lemon juice, and honey to sweeten. It was supposed to be good for the blood. I would never have dreamed of drinking it in my own pregnancy. But I have learned since then that it is rich in iron, folic acid, vitamin C and B vitamins.

A woman brings to a daughter's pregnancy her own experience of birth. This may be stated overtly, 'All the women in our family have premature ruptured membranes', 'I was three days in labour with you. I don't expect you'll have it easy', or, more happily, 'You've got wide hips like me. I enjoyed my births.' Or she may hide distressing birth memories, pushing them into the back of her mind, refusing to dwell on them, resisting any talk about birth because, 'It's different nowadays' or 'You're in good hands'.

When I was expecting my first child my mother was quite open with me about her long, painful labours – which she met with courage and a deep spiritual conviction that she was honoured to be able to give life. She had her two babies at home in her own bed with my father holding her hand. As she laboured with me there was a woodpecker working away on a tree outside the window. Faced with what looked like an impossible task, it persisted, hour after hour, in pecking at the wood. The bird kept her going through a labour that lasted a night, a day, and another night. My mother was very small, but gave birth to babies of more than nine pounds. I knew that if she could do it, I could do it.

Pregnant women sometimes say that they cannot discuss birth with their mothers. They are even less likely to do so with their mothers-in-law. 'She never talks about things like that,' they say, and they sometimes add, 'I think she must have had a bad time.' They are often aware of a mother's negative birth experience though she has never referred to it and believes that they know nothing about it. Suffering endured in childbirth, the experience which many women have of being totally disempowered, may go unresolved for many years, for far from quickly forgetting their birth experiences, women carry with them their memories of them until they die. There are many grandmothers who still suffer the trauma of birth in which they were disempowered and abused, but had no language to give voice to the experience because it was all explained in medical terms and as being necessary for the baby's sake.

For women who have given birth to a child with a genetic disability, or have experienced the death of a child, the announcement of a daughter's pregnancy gives rise to mingled fear and hope. Fifty years ago everyone accepted that, sadly, some children were not 'normal' and nothing could be done about it. Now women are expected to have antenatal screening for anomalies – amniocentesis, blood tests, ultrasound scans – so that defective babies can be aborted. This produces new ethical dilemmas and new anxieties for individuals and families. A grandmother who is aware that she may have passed on a genetic disease or disability, such as cystic fibrosis or Down's syndrome, or an inherited trait like dwarfism, bears a heavy burden of knowledge, doubt and guilt. After a heart murmur had been detected in her baby grandson one woman wrote, 'Our eldest son died ten years ago. He collapsed during a game of football at his school. He was thirteen years old and the cause of his death was a rare muscle defect. You can imagine how we feel. The death of my son is a sorrow that never goes away. This little grandson has brought something of Francis back into my life.' But the question is always there: will this child die too?

A daughter's pregnancy brings renewed and hidden grieving for a woman who has had a traumatic birth experience. Yet it also presents a fresh opportunity to come to terms with bad birth memories, to learn more about how women's bodies work in child-bearing, and how other people's attitudes and actions can affect the physiological process and the emotional experience, negatively or positively. A woman can borrow the books her daughter is reading and attend classes and discussion groups with her. In this way a daughter's pregnancy can be an enabling experience for a grandmother, while at the same time she gives her daughter strong, confident emotional support. In a society where birth has been turned into a medical crisis an expectant mother often yearns for such woman-to-woman support. It is the kind of support which implies or states openly, 'Of course you can do it. You are strong!', 'It is your choice. It's your body and your baby', 'You don't have to be a "good girl". If that is what you want, insist on it', 'I don't know about that, but let's find out', and which helps her plan ahead. It is support which accepts that the woman may change her mind, and that she can change her doctor, her hospital, her place of birth, and that she has a right to do this. It is support which puts the pregnant woman in control, but which also accepts that there are certain situations in which she may make the decision to surrender control.

When a woman does this it is empowering for her as well as for her daughter. Anxious women have come with their daughters to my antenatal discussion groups. The daughter often invited her mother because she felt that this fear could contaminate her pregnancy, and hoped that it might be exorcised by knowledge. The mothers have usually been reluctant at first to talk openly about their experiences because, 'You don't talk about things like that do you? Not to pregnant women. It might have a terrible effect.' They sat quietly watching while we discussed things we had heard about other women's birth experiences. I asked, 'What are the worst things that you can imagine happening to you in birth?' And then we explored together their deepest fears. We discussed how they wanted to handle pain, how childbirth pain is the by-product of powerful muscles working and the pressure of the ball of the baby's head in its descent, and we talked about the pharmacological techniques and self-help skills that can eradicate or ease this pain. Then the grandmothers started sharing their experiences, talked about what they went through, and those in the group suggested how their births could have been different, how people could have helped instead of hindered, the things they needed but never got, the setting for birth, and – above all – the difference between feeling in control and feeling utterly helpless. In this way these expectant grandmothers have contributed a great deal to my discussion groups, and have often come out of them with a sigh of relief that at last they have been able to face up to their terrible birth experiences and to resolve the trauma.

A woman may feel confused about what she should do to support a pregnant daughter who is on the journey from being a daughter to her mother to being a mother to her own child. That transition can be difficult. Sometimes she seems like a little girl; at other times she seeks to be independent of her mother. In a pregnancy journal Ellen Judith Reich records how upset she was when her mother was talking about going on holiday to Papua New Guinea or perhaps to Turkey around the time the baby was due. Everyone assumed that her mother would be excited and supportive. Yet here she was planning a holiday when the baby was going to be born. Ellen had already told her mother that she and Rick wanted the first week or so on their own. 'I'm astounded. Bereft . . . I guessed I still wanted her around, for questions on the phone and to come down anyway, early, if I changed my mind. And anger, I feel that too. Her *only* daughter giving birth to her *first* child and Mom's first grandchild to boot. Almost total disbelief on my part. Don't you *care*?' She is highly critical of her mother when she feels she is not living her own life. Now that her mother is doing what *she* wants, she feels rejected. She asks herself whether her mother loves her, 'Does she love my baby? Does she even believe my baby will exist?'[2]

A grandmother may be caught in a double bind. Should she stay around, eager to be involved, agog for news, ready to rush to her daughter's side with love, sympathy, flowers and champagne? Or ensure that she is busily occupied elsewhere, so that her daughter feels free of maternal encumbrances and the couple can share a peak experience in their lives without anyone else intruding? Or are neither of these courses of action quite what the younger woman really wants? Her daughter may not be sure whether, once labour starts, she will need her there or not, but would like her ready to come at a moment's notice if she decides she wants her. The only way to deal with this situation is to be completely open, to lay your cards on the table and say clearly, 'I can do *this* or I can do *that*. It is up to you to tell me what you prefer. We need to discuss this. I will respect your decisions, but if you change your mind I'll try to fit in with whatever you want at the time.'

Grandmothers at birth

In many cultures it is unthinkable that a grandmother should not be present at the birth of her grandchild. It is taken for granted that a daughter returns to her mother's home to give birth or that the father's mother is present. In fact, the word for 'midwife' is often 'Granny', 'Grandy' or 'Nana'. Though the grandmother might not be the woman who catches the baby, and another older woman takes on that role, in traditional societies midwives are often thought of as grandmothers. Granny midwives still deliver some babies in the Southern states of the USA and catch most babies in traditional societies, where women do not have access to hospitals, and where even if they do, they dislike the impersonality, cultural disruption and inappropriateness of hospital care, or are forced to make long journeys from rural areas in order to reach a hospital. Rather than being young women who have often not had babies themselves, in most societies midwives are older women who have the status of grandmothers in the community, and who have large families of children and grandchildren.

Yet whether or not they have had children, these midwives always had grandmother status. In a book which records oral history from the handywoman to the professional midwife Nicky Leap and Billie Hunter tell the story of Granny Anderson, a Tyneside midwife in the 1920s. 'If your mother sent you for Granny Anderson, you used to run like the clappers up the back lane to get to her. And your house had to be spotlessly clean before she'd enter. Scrubbed out with carbolic . . . She used to give you a list of what had to be ready or to hand, like torn sheets, piles of newspapers and boiling water – because nobody had running water . . . And there was always a bowl of hot water and carbolic soap for Granny Anderson to wash her hands in – that was one of the musts.'[3] When trained midwives first started to work they often met resistance from families. One who worked in Battersea said she was allowed very little boiling water because births were usually handled by grandmothers.[4]

As birth became medicalized doctors took charge of maternity care, granny midwives were reviled and birth was moved from home to hospital. This did not happen in a uniform way throughout the Western world, and hospital birth was the norm in the USA before the Second World War. But it did not become the norm in Britain till the 1960s. In a study of home birth in Ireland, Marie O'Connor reveals that in Gaelic parts of Donegal in the 1940s the language of childbirth was understood only by women.[5] Men had nothing to do with it and did not even know the appropriate words. It was the husband's mother who served as birth attendant, not the woman's mother. In the sixties the tradition persisted of having a local midwife, helped by the mother-in-law and female neighbours, who brought in soup and took away the washing. Grandmother help in childbirth ceased abruptly with the concentration of virtually all births in large hospitals in the late seventies. Shivaun's birth story is unusual. She had her first baby in hospital and disliked the experience. When she went into labour at a hospital antenatal clinic she thought she had better get home, so she left the clinic, caught a bus, walked three miles to her house, and with the help of her mother-in-law and a neighbour, had the baby an hour later.[6]

For most women today birth has become an ordeal to be endured in an alien environment among strangers. Aware of this, midwives are trying to recreate many of the qualities of care that the granny midwives offered: personal relationships with clients, awareness of the social context of women's lives, open communication, and a setting for birth which enables the woman to trust and work with her body.

For any woman who goes to the hospital and sits outside the room where her daughter is giving birth, unable to do anything to help, the birth is likely to be highly stressful. One woman, who had experienced difficult labours herself, wrote about her feelings as she sat right outside the delivery room while her daughter was in labour. 'A woman in the throes of labour just screamed "Nurse! Nurse! Help me!" There are feelings that are off-limit, that I push away, that I don't allow myself to dwell on. That's not her screaming. I'll close the door. I can't stand the thought of my daughter suffering. I love her so much . . . This baby is taking a very long time to arrive. I am just sitting, sitting, sitting . . . Come on, baby!'

Another grandmother rushed to the hospital when her daughter was admitted a month before the baby was due because her blood pressure had shot up. 'Induction was tried over a twenty-four-hour period, without result. I spent much of this time at the hospital, and went home to sleep, or try to. The phone rang just after midnight. Sally had an emergency Caesarean as the baby began to show signs of distress, and Alexander weighed four pounds twelve ounces. I went to hospital next morning. My husband joined me. Poor Sally looked so ill, and we were only allowed a few minutes. Yet holding her newborn grandchild in her arms was a peak experience, something she remembered with a physical thrill of pleasure.

Being present at the birth of a grandchild can be a happy and deeply satisfying experience. A woman whose daughter had a Caesarean section at her first birth was able to attend the second birth, which took place at home. She had been invited to look after the three year old so that her son-in-law could be free to support his wife. She and the older child were in the room together and witnessed the birth of the baby. She says it was 'glorious', a never-to-be forgotten experience.

Another grandmother was anxious when she learned that

her daughter was exploring the possibility of a home birth and that both she and her husband were invited to be there. She said she was very afraid because, 'homebirths were like going backwards. I was fearful of complications.' The daughter invited her to a discussion with the two midwives. This did not convince her, but she respected her decision. Four days before she went into labour her daughter had contractions on and off, and her mother hoped that she would decide to go into hospital after all. But she stayed at home. 'The miracle finally happened.' She was surprised and delighted at how fully involved she was in the birth of her grandchild. She found herself part of a loving birthing community, united in giving support to her daughter. 'It was a beautiful experience.'

Being a birth companion may mean just being there, quietly watching and waiting. Your daughter may want you to help in practical ways, or she may want her partner to be her main support, and your task may turn out to be offering quiet back-up. Only at the time will it be clear exactly what your role should be. It could be to give emotional support to her partner, for example, taking over with back-rubbing if he gets tired or needs a break, communicating confidence and reinforcing him in his role. If he becomes anxious or over-stressed it may be that he needs to get outside in the fresh air, to have a snack or take a brief nap. After hours of long, weary labour your daughter may be worrying about him and be glad that someone is considering his needs, too. On the other hand, she may feel that she cannot go on if he goes out of the room, and if you suggest that he should, you are intruding on their relationship and on the understanding between them. Be sensitive to what the birthing woman wants and avoid imposing your own ideas. Above all, she should be in control.

Giving support could entail responsibility for a grandchild, explaining what is happening, why his mother is making a noise: huffing and puffing, grunting, shouting or groaning. 'It's very hard work . . . She's pushing the baby down to be born', and quietly explaining that the round, wrinkled object like a large walnut is the top of the baby's head, and describing the placenta and its life-giving task. You can get some ideas about words and praises to use from a book of mine written for children, *Being Born*.[7] You may want to obtain this book before the baby is born to tell the story of pregnancy and birth, so that the child is well-prepared and can voice any fears or anxieties.

Here are some ideas that may be useful if your daughter wants you to do things to help her, especially if she has no one else with her to help in this particular way:

- Offer her sips of water whenever she wishes. A bendy straw enables her to drink easily if she is on all fours or lying on her side.
- Give her small ice cubes to suck.
- Brush her hair slowly.
- Refresh her with a cold face-cloth or compress laid on her forehead or at the nape of her neck.
- Help her move to more comfortable positions so that she is upright or semi-upright, and ones in which her pelvis is free to circle and rock. Use pillows, furniture or your own body to support her so that she can follow the rhythms of her body in a birth 'dance'.
- Fill and refill a hot water bottle if she likes heat against her lower back or shoulders.
- Massage her shoulders or feet with firm, slow strokes of fingers and thumbs, and the small of her back with heels of your palms or your fists, leaning your own weight down through your arms so that the pressure goes really deep.
- Cradle her head in your hands and support her shoulders firmly.
- Tell her she is doing well. Give her your quiet confidence. Smile.

Some women do not want to be touched in labour, because the energy inside them is so strong. Others long to be held, stroked and massaged. Be sensitive as to whether or not your daughter wants to be touched, whether she wants you in her line of vision and likes to make eye contact during contractions or to close her eyes, and whether she welcomes verbal encouragement or would prefer you to be silent.

In early labour she may like light, easily digested snacks to keep up her strength. If labour is long you and her partner should remember to eat something yourselves.

When a grandmother has not experienced birth herself, either because she had an elective Caesarean section with general anaesthesia or because her child was adopted, being invited to attend a daughter's birth may be very challenging and stimulate in her conflicting emotions and much deep thought. A woman who was adopted at the age of six says of her mother, 'It's always been a very close relationship. The only thing that has been missing is that she was not there when I was born.' Her mother told me, 'I was really quite frightened. How would I be? How would I feel if she was in pain? And I was also very thrilled and tremendously honoured. I couldn't have asked *my* mother because there was a big physical barrier between us. I wouldn't have wanted her to come into the room when I was on the bed pan, for instance. The reason that Bryony wanted me to share the birth experience with her was that I had missed out on it.' Bryony and her husband talked this through at length first of all and worked out exactly what her mother's role should be during the labour, and that it should be distinct from her husband's. His first reaction had been to ask, 'What am I going to do then?' It turned out that the labour was prolonged, difficult, and highly 'managed'. Bryony had an epidural and, as her mother says, 'It was all very anxious because nothing seemed to be happening . . . It was wonderful to see the little head. But she didn't cry. I was very anxious.' Bryony caught sight of a 'very blue-looking baby' who was immediately taken off to be resuscitated, and her mother stayed with her, holding her hand, while her husband followed the baby to watch while she was sucked out and bagged. 'She was a great support for both of us.' Bryony's mother said that once all was well Bryony was 'radiant', and she went home 'walking on air'. One significant element in this birth experience is that, though the labour was highly 'managed', there was anxiety when it was discovered that the baby had passed meconium (the first contents of the bowels and a sign that the baby may be short of oxygen). When the baby was born 'flat' (limp, blue and not breathing well), this grandmother had a defined function, knew exactly what she could do to help, and her presence was fully accepted by the midwives, so that she felt part of a team and was never shut out from having full information.

In many hospitals it is difficult to guarantee this, and

grandmothers are themselves traumatized by an environment which is repressive and in which care fails to meet the needs and wishes of the woman and her family. So if you plan to be with your daughter ensure that this is on record in a letter or birth plan beforehand; whenever possible meet the staff who will be giving care; and learn as much as you can about the process of birth and exactly what your daughter wants of her birth companions and the professionals caring for her.

For a woman whose daughter was adopted, being able to share in the preparation for and experience of childbirth and the warm sensuousness of a new-born baby brings a delight which may be completely unexpected, 'That lovely feeling of skin and the scent of a baby in my arms!' A woman whose daughter was adopted says that she rejoices in her daughter being able to do what she could not manage herself: 'There is something magic about it.'

Birth can be a healing, enriching and empowering experience for a grandmother.

Moving closer, moving apart

For many mothers and daughters pregnancy and birth bring a new closeness and understanding. This is dependent on their being able to meet regularly face to face, without having to be 'on show', crowded by other family members, or trying to cram everything into an occasional brief encounter. There needs to be ongoing dialogue.

A woman says of her daughter, a successful business woman with a life very different from her mother's, who has now had her first baby, 'Holly hugs me a lot, where she used to give me just a daughterly kiss on the cheek. I feel that she has let me in. Not even let me in, but beckoned me in, enfolded me in her family in a very close way.' Holly told her mother that she felt differently toward her now. She asked her how. 'You know perfectly well, I'm a lot nicer.' 'How do you mean – nicer?' 'I'm much gentler, aren't I? I'm softer.' 'And she is,' her mother says. 'It's that old cliché that with the love and commitment that you feel for your baby, you suddenly realise the love that has been given to you over the years – love you previously took for granted.' A new mother starts to understand why her mother worried about her when she was late, and stayed up waiting for her.

Joy in the baby is shared between the two women and they are bonded more firmly in the strength of their love for this child. As each shows her pleasure in the baby, the other's joy is intensified. 'She wants me around in a way she didn't before. Not as a prop, not as a source of advice or reassurance, but because, she says, she feels closer to me than any other woman in her life.'

As they get nearer each other they leap the barriers that divide the generations. A daughter relates to her mother not only as a daughter but as a woman who has been through the same transition. Suddenly they are women sharing in the way that all women passing through the same life experience are able to do. They discover sisterhood: 'I feel she sees me for the first time as a woman, not just her mother.'

But the opposite sometimes happens. A mother and daughter move further away from each other. It may be that a woman enters enthusiastically into her grandmother role and abdicates her role as a mother. A daughter who needs emotional support on the roller-coaster journey of the difficult weeks and months after birth, but does not get it, feels bereft. All the attention and love is given to the baby, with none at all left for her. As a woman talked about the birth of a grandchild, she remembered that this is how it was when her son was born. She felt that her mother instantly became a grandmother and less of a mother to her. Her son has just become a father. 'I would never want him to think that I loved him less now or regarded him simply as the baby's father. In fact, I am taking a lot of delight in watching the changes in my son as a result of being a partner and father.'

A grandmother is bound to feel rejected if she expects too much of or romanticizes her special bond with a grandchild. When a baby is in a close and exclusive relationship with his mother she may feel shut out too. She longs to hold, cuddle and do things for the baby, but he is fixed like a limpet to his mother's breast – and she is an outsider. This is one reason why a grandmother may try to persuade her daughter to switch to formula, or at least to supplement with a bottle. She wants the baby for herself. She yearns to relive the sensual pleasures of mothering. A grandmother who recognized that she felt like this told me, 'From the age of four months to seven years he would not allow anyone but his parents to handle him. This has created an emotional problem for me.' She feels rejected by the child, and relegated by his parents to being merely a detached observer of his development.

Unhappiness after childbirth

For many women the transition to motherhood, especially after the birth of a first baby, is difficult. If you think back to how you felt as a new mother – and can be honest about it – you may remember that it was not all unalloyed pleasure for you either. We tend to gloss over the times of unhappiness as we look back at those early days of motherhood through the rosy mists of memory. A woman is most likely to be unhappy when she is isolated from loving, supportive relationships, and her misery results in further isolation.

After having a baby it is common for women to feel that they have lost something precious, and they need time to grieve over this. It is a normal transitional emotional state, and it may occur, for men as well as women, in other life passages, such as after losing a job, retirement, or moving house. A new mother is expected to be fulfilled and contented, so this unaccountable sense of loss forces her to put on an act, playing a happy mother with her baby. The loss may be that of the close, intimate relationship with her lover, loss of oneself as a child – who now has to grow up and take responsibility for another human being, loss of a body which was a girl's and has now become a woman's, loss of the comfort of the baby inside, loss of the fantasy baby – who was very different from the one expected, or loss of the self as a person who is confident, capable and able to control events. This is one reason why the weeks and months after birth are often a time of emotional upheaval.

One way of looking at depression is to consider it as *inturned anger* – anger that it is too dangerous to express. When anger is blocked because we feel that we have no right to it, or that it would upset other people too much and result, perhaps, in a withdrawal of love, or we are frightened of being punished in some other way, it is turned against the self.

A characteristic of depression after birth, as with depression in any other major life transition, is that you are separated from everyone else as if by a glass wall. A depressed new mother often feels that she is not, and never can be, a good enough mother, and she may withdraw from the baby as well as other people and be afraid of harming the child. She may suffer a sense of impending doom – that she will die, for instance, and feel that it would be better for everyone if she did.

If a daughter or daughter-in-law is severely depressed a grandmother may have to give the baby the love and care the mother is incapable of giving. But her daughter needs her too. She needs the reassurance of the older woman's unwavering love. It may be difficult to give that if her daughter is clearly not coping, and a grandmother often feels bewildered and angry because she does not understand what is happening, especially if she has never herself suffered from depression. The temptation is to snap, 'Pull yourself together!' or to tell her to count her blessings, and concentrate on looking after the baby. Yet when a woman is this unhappy, having other people take over the baby may seem proof that she is a complete failure as a mother. She feels even more abnormal and rejected as she sees her mother giving love to the baby. For some women this is a recurring theme in the unhappiness – 'She never loved me that way' – and the grandmother feels unfairly accused while she is trying to do all in her power to help.

When a woman feels like this she needs a chance to express her resentment and hostility toward her mother, her doubts about herself, and often, too, her resentment of the baby, without risking recrimination, and in an atmosphere of total acceptance. A postnatal discussion or psychotherapy group focused on the challenges facing new parents, or one-to-one counselling, enables her to do this in a safe setting. The GP or health visitor can help with a referral to appropriate agencies. Sometimes the hard shell of resentment cracks open and a woman accuses her mother of not loving her, not caring for her in ways she needed, and of having failed her as a mother. Painful as it is, it is important to listen, and to acknowledge that, however unreal the criticism seems to be, *her feelings are real*.

A woman who has recently had a baby may want to talk about a difficult birth over and over again. This often happens after weeks or months when she appears to have put it behind her. She is trying to come to terms with an experience which, however easy and straightforward it may have seemed to other people, was traumatic for her – because she was disempowered. She is anxious, stressed, finds it difficult to concentrate, is sometimes hectically active, and may have sudden panic attacks, nightmares, and waking flashbacks to the birth, which are much more intense than memories, because she feels that it is happening to her all over again. Here again, it is vital to listen and to accept – to validate how she feels rather than produce counter-arguments, to acknowledge and mirror her emotions rather than try to explain why a Caesarean section or induced labour was necessary, for example. To be disempowered in childbirth is a terrifying experience. A woman feels trapped, defenceless, physically and emotionally exposed, and often sexually abused and mutilated. Recollection of the ordeal she endured may sweep over her in waves of panic.

Post-traumatic stress is different from depression – though it may be an element in depression. Many soldiers in Vietnam, not only Americans but Vietnamese also, suffered trauma of this kind after being helpless in situations of extreme violence and horror. Anyone who witnesses a serious road accident, fire or bomb explosion may experience similar post-traumatic stress. Even when a woman has a beautiful and thriving baby, but things have been done to her in childbirth over which she had no control, and even when she has suffered no physical damage (episiotomy and suturing of her perineum or an operative delivery, for example), she may be emotionally damaged by the experience.

It takes patience, compassion and emotional resilience to help a woman through such pain. She cannot just let it go, however much she wants to. If your daughter or daughter-in-law is struggling to cope with an experience of this kind do not treat her as a child. She does not want to be babied. Listen to her in *sisterhood*, as another woman who knows how it is to have other people, usually powerful men, manage our bodies and decide what is to happen to them.

She may come to a point when she wants to take positive action – to find out exactly what occurred and why, during a birth which for her was all muddle and confusion. She may want to confront her oppressors and take legal action. She may seek therapy. It is very likely that she wants to reach out and help other women, so that they do not have to go through a similar experience, and join with others to improve the maternity services. Whatever she decides, she needs your support and understanding.

The absent grandmother

The birth of a baby often intensifies mourning for a mother who has died. During pregnancy mourning tends to be put on hold. When a woman's mother has died before or during the pregnancy she is often so focused on the baby inside that it has to be delayed until after the birth. Then grief really hits her, and may be overwhelming. Before the baby was born it was a *daughter* who mourned. Now it is as a *mother* that she mourns, too – that her child cannot know his grandmother, and that she is not there to delight in her grandchild. Jill's mother died five years before she had her first baby. 'I didn't realise how much I would miss her. It came as a shock. I went through the grieving all over again. I thought of how she would cuddle the baby, how proud and happy she would have been.' Then she said, 'It's ridiculous, because if I'm honest I'm sure we would have disagreed about almost everything'.

A woman whose mother died when she was seventeen dreamed, during her pregnancy, of giving birth to a daughter and then doing all the things that her mother was never able to do with her because she had been more or less bedridden for years. At the same, she was anxious that she might have no maternal feelings and that she would not know how to mother. She feared dying and 'abandoning' her child, as she herself had been deserted. 'The thought of dying young and leaving a child motherless is so terrifying to me that it is almost justification for not having one at all.'[8] Another woman writes, 'My mother died when I was ten and I had always harbored the fantasy that if only I could become a mother, my mother would come back.' When her mother did not return she mourned for her anew, and the first eight weeks after the birth were filled with grief. Hope Edelman, writing about motherless daughters, comments that 'parenting often doubles as self-parenting when a mother still longs to be mothered.' A woman who has lost her mother often feels whole again when she has a child of her own. The birth of the baby enables her to rediscover her own childhood.

But it does not always work like that. Annie's mother had a long illness and then died when she was still a child. She expected her baby to be a girl. She was shocked when it turned out to be a son. 'I felt cheated. I felt robbed.' Hope Edelman says, 'For twenty-nine years Annie had been planning to recreate her childhood and give it the happy ending it deserved ... The script was already written and Annie knew her part. All she needed was the little girl who would play her as a child.'[9] When a baby does not come up to expectations because it does not match a new mother's fantasies it can be very painful for a grandmother, especially if the younger woman seems to be rejecting or neglecting the baby.

When her own mother has died but her partner's mother is alive a woman may compare the mother-in-law with her own mother – sometimes with very idealised memories of how she remembers her. She resents the fact that her partner's mother is alive and can enjoy the baby, while her own mother is dead. Even a mother-in-law who is loving and sensitive can never be allowed to take the place of her missing mother. To do so would be a kind of treachery.

When a grandmother picks up resentment from a daughter-in-law whose mother has died, and there are undertones of hostility that she feels she has not deserved, it may be that the younger woman is grieving over her mother's death. This can happen not only when her mother has died recently, but many years afterwards.

A woman can discover her mother-in-law as a friend who listens in a non-judgemental and reflective way, without intrusive comments, as she gradually finds that it is safe to talk with her about her life, her childhood experiences, and – perhaps very tentatively at first – what mothering and being mothered means to her. The important thing is to respect and validate how she feels. The love and understanding a grandmother gives can be healing.

Falling in Love

When your first grandchild is put in your arms you may be overwhelmed with love. The intensity and depth of emotion felt for this little human being comes as a surprise to many women. A woman whose grandson was born four weeks pre-term by Caesarean section says, 'My son put this tiny scrap into my arms; he was wrapped in two blankets, wore woolly mittens and hat. I was completely knocked out, overwhelmed by the great rush of emotion as I looked at him. I loved him immediately and powerfully with an intensity that was so unexpected.' A woman suddenly remembers how it was to see and to touch her own new-born baby. As this baby's eyes open on a new world and she gazes into their violet depths, she is swept back in time to the first few heady days of motherhood.

With this comes, too, the sense that you are part of the great tree of life extending way back in the past and on into the future. This feeling is accentuated if a parent is dying or has recently died. A woman whose father was terminally ill as her first grandchild was born says, 'I felt, "He is going and Hannah has arrived." I gained insight into the scheme of things.' The birth of a grandchild brings a deeply satisfying sense of continuity. 'There are amazing feelings of connection to life, to time past, present and future', 'My baby has had a baby. The circle is complete.' Over and over again women use the term *circles*: 'You have the feeling that you live again through your children becoming parents. It puts it all in perspective. The love goes right through. It makes a circle.' You relive your own precious passed experiences as a mother and complete the circle.

More than 2000 years ago the Greek philosopher Heraclitus expressed his sense of the connectedness of all things,

> Out of life comes death,
> and out of death, life.
> Out of the young, the old

and out of the old, the young.
Out of waking, sleep,
and out of sleep, waking.

The stream of creation and dissolution never stops.

Granny Trouble

If you experience problems in a relationship with a daughter or daughter-in-law it may help to think about how she sees you, and whether she is seeking something in the relationship that is missing, or why she may be put on the defensive by your behaviour and the ways in which you communicate with her. Could you be the woman who insists on giving sweets that ruin your grandchild's teeth, who 'spoils' the baby, or tries to potty train a one year old when your daughter has decided that the baby will be clean in his own time? Do you cling to what your daughter or daughter-in-law considers outmoded ideas of child-rearing and education?

In discussion groups during pregnancy, couples often express apprehension about how either or both of the grandmothers are going to be once there is a baby: 'How shall we deal with Mother?' The man may be anxious to protect the woman from her mother and make sure that she does not interfere, and she is anxious that her mother might upset her partner. She may also want to convince his mother that she is a good enough wife and mother, 'She's worried that I am going to neglect him when we have the baby and that he won't be fed properly or be able to do his work, which is very demanding'; 'Mother worries all the time about how well I'm feeling. She's too solicitous. I couldn't bear to have her around when the baby's born'; 'I know that Martin won't feel it's really his home if she comes to stay, and yet I realise that she's feeling shut out'; 'We have to hide the car round the back of the house because Mother says I shouldn't be driving while I am pregnant'; 'Her mother is the dominating type'; 'Roger would like to opt out and leave me with my mother, but I am grown up now and I need him, not her. How can I get him to see this?'; 'His mum thinks that I'm too young and I don't think she is going to trust me to do right by his baby. She is checking up on me almost every day as it is – asking what we had for dinner, seeing if the kitchen's clean, criticising my housekeeping in a roundabout way'; 'She's a very busy lady, Ruth's mother, and she likes to organise things. I'm having to put my foot down'; 'Mother has been dropping so many hints for such a long time about when are we going to start a family that I don't feel it's our baby any more'.

Following family reunions I often have urgent requests to help with breast-feeding, or there are distress signals connected with anxiety about the baby and the woman's ability to mother. Unfortunately, when grandmothers come to stay the unintended outcome may be that a new mother, especially a first-time mother, is disabled rather than enabled by the visit. Easter and Christmas are peak periods for mothers to lose their confidence and need someone with whom they can talk. The stresses and strains of mother and mother-in-law visits may continue in the months and years that follow and though conflicts are often resolved in time, in some families they become a permanent part of the scene.

Grandmothers are often bewildered by this. They are trying to help, struggling not to criticize when they long to speak, leaving the young couple their space, giving of their love – doing all these things – but somehow they get it wrong.

Conflicts about discipline

Thirty-three mothers of young children (mostly under ten years old) told me about difficulties in their relationships with their mothers or partners' mothers. The vast majority were concerned about conflicting attitudes to discipline. This included disagreements about how to deal with tantrums and bad manners, children's food behaviour, toilet training, what to do when a child is disobedient, and the case for positive reinforcement as opposed to coercion and punishment. Mothers, on the whole, favour a relaxed attitude, are quick to pick up a crying baby or comfort a distressed child, and do not expect instant obedience. They believe in discussion and explanation or, with the youngest children, distraction, and believe that children learn to be considerate of others if they are themselves respected and treated with consideration. They tend to be critical of rigid, authoritarian systems of child-rearing, of threats and physical punishment, and of withdrawal of love. There are often fundamental disagreements between mothers and grandmothers on these matters, grandmothers usually advocating a firm framework and more control over children's behaviour.

A mother of a baby a few months old says that her mother tells her she is 'spoiling' the baby by 'kissing and cuddling her all the time. We should leave her in her room by herself, even if she cries, and feed her by the clock.' Another says her mother-in-law 'believes children should be seen and not heard and should sit in one place and not do anything'. She also thinks they should be 'bottle-fed, smacked and toilet-trained by six months. (I would love to know if she was ever successful with her own kids as none of them want much to do with her now!)' This mother-in-law sounds rather like another who 'believes babies should be seen and not heard, drugged (with Vallergen) if they cry "for no reason", and are easily spoiled by cuddling and demand feeding, that it is good for them to have "hate times" (when they're distraught) every day, and that they wet their nappies deliberately to get attention'. This woman adds that the older woman 'learnt her baby care in books printed in the 1950s, and won't budge'. Sometimes a grandmother hated the time when she had young children, felt trapped by motherhood, and worries that her daughter will suffer in the same way. She wants to make it easier for her, so she criticizes what she is doing and tries to organize her life. One woman says, 'My mother resented, indeed loathed, having children herself and she cannot understand my joy and contentment.' The baby cries every time this granny holds her. She says the baby is spoiled and should be fed by the clock. She believes that children should be ignored whenever possible, and is adamant that physical punishment is the only effective form of discipline.

A woman told me that she cannot trust her mother to be a loving grandmother. The older woman is highly critical of the freedom and spontaneous affection in her daughter's home. The result is that she dare not leave the children with her. She explains it by saying that her mother's mother was a strict disciplinarian, who often employed physical punishment and had a streak of cruelty. She remembers her grandmother giving her sweets and then punishing her for being greedy.

'She always favoured my older sister and would lock me in a room while she played with her.' So she is sorry for her mother, who obviously had a deprived childhood, and is determined to break the continuum of unhappiness in the family, and create a warm and loving home for her children.

Grandmothers who see babies as potential tyrants who have to be tamed if they are to fit in with family life often worry that a son will be neglected, or that a marriage will break up, if the baby is not disciplined. 'When Erin was only three weeks old she was arguing that she should be made to wait for four hours between feeds in order to give me time to myself. I can't understand how the extra time to yourself you may or may not gain from making a baby wait such a long time would be worth while if the baby is wailing with hunger. But she believes babies can be "selfish" about their food – wanting too much time on the breast and taking too long to feed.' The couple have talked about this together and worked out a strategy to deal with his mother. 'My partner often says that he has more problems managing his "spoiled" parents than the possibility of a spoilt baby daughter.'

On the other hand, there are grandmothers who take more liberal views while the daughters or daughters-in-law insist on 'good behaviour', believe that 'a quick smack does wonders', criticize the older woman for laughing at or colluding with naughtiness, being a 'softie', refusing to back them up in their attempts at discipline, and for letting children 'get away with murder'. They say they cannot control the children's behaviour when granny has gone. These women often complain that when *they* were children their mothers were not this relaxed and indulgent. They resent the fact that the older woman is more gentle, tolerant and loving with her grandchild than they remember her being as a mother, 'She was extremely strict when I was a child. She is extremely over-indulgent with my children. She spoils them rotten. Once they are back home the rules change and they are not the centre of existence any more. One thing I can't handle is when I ask my mum not to do something with my kids that I don't agree with and she ignores me and does it anyway. It makes me furious!' This woman adds, 'She's a very loving grandmother, but she didn't seem to be that way with me, and certainly isn't with *me* now.'

Rejected daughters

Another major element that emerges in these younger women's accounts is that some feel rejected by their mothers, and very lonely and unloved as they try to rear their children. They long for understanding and sympathy. Sometimes it is just that a grandmother lives far away and is out of touch. But there are grandmothers who live close by but carefully keep their distance, so that there is little communication between mother and daughter, and the younger woman feels isolated. And there are other grandmothers who are on hand but spend most of their time expressing disapproval and criticism.

A woman with two small daughters says, 'I desperately wanted a girl. My mother said, "You don't want a girl. They only grow up to be little bitches" (meaning teenage years). That comment really hurt. I found out a few months ago that my mother wanted a boy for her first child and that she did not breast-feed me, but did breast-feed my brothers.' The daughter now feels totally rejected. 'My mum had a mother who would phone every day and had to know the ins and outs of her daughter's life. She resented this and said she would never do it to *her* children.' As a result this grandmother rarely visits or phones and displays a complete lack of interest in her daughter's life and in her grandchildren.

Even when a grandmother visits frequently her daughter may be ignored, because granny concentrates on the children. 'My mother has become so obsessed by my children that now I take second place. My feelings and our conversations are always secondary to what our children are doing.' Another woman says, 'My mother and I were best friends before the birth of my daughter. She was always interested in everything I did and said and always caring. We always have done things together and gone places together. This changed dramatically when I gave birth. Mum didn't seem to be as concerned for my welfare as much as my daughter's. She would visit to see my daughter and forget to kiss me good-bye as she was too wrapped up in the baby.'

A number of women who talked to me about their mothers

and mothers-in-law felt neglected in the months after the birth. The time after a baby is born is one when many women long for their own mothers to give emotional support, to validate them in their role as mothers, and to offer help in a practical, down-to-earth way. New mothers still in their early twenties may seek a relationship of some dependency before they have the self-confidence to enjoy being independent. Knowing exactly when to give help and when to withdraw is a tricky business for a grandmother. If she is to do the right thing she has to be available when needed, and unobtrusive when she is not. There are no instant formulas for success. The simplest and most honest approach is to let your daughter know that you realize that there are times when she would welcome your help and other times when she wants privacy and independence and ask her to be open with you about it. Many mothers and daughters find it difficult to talk this way, but if you do not discuss the issues there are bound to be misunderstandings which hurt you both. One woman says, 'Mum and dad are often whispering and looking at each other. They sit in disgust for me leaving Stephanie to feed herself, making a mess. But my mum never expresses her ideas, only turns her nose up and is silent.'

In the weeks immediately following birth many mothers do not wish their mothers to be involved in their honeymoon time with the baby. They want to demonstrate that they can make independent decisions, and can cope alone or with the loving companionship and active fatherhood of their partners. Then even the most altruistically motivated help, the most loving concern for them, may be wrong. The daughter also believes that it is difficult for her mother to be a loving grandmother and accept the freedom and spontaneous affection in her daughter's home because her own mother was a strict disciplinarian who often employed physical punishment, and had a streak of cruelty.

Feeding the child

Feeding and feeding behaviour is a major topic of disagreement. Remembering her own childhood, one woman says,

'My mother was very strict with food. Every scrap had to be eaten off your plate before you could leave the table. I often fell asleep face first into my plate late at night because she would not let me leave the table because of some food left on my plate. We would get lectures about starving refugees and told "waste not want not" until it rung in your ears. As a result I am a compulsive eater.' It is only recently that she has stopped making herself ill by eating too much because she feels she must empty her plate or eat all the food laid out on the table. 'If my child eats – fine, and if he doesn't eat much I know he won't pass out from hunger before his next meal.'

Many disagreements between daughters and their mothers or mothers-in-law are about infant feeding. Grandmothers tend to be less confident about the value of breast-feeding and are often anxious that babies are not putting on weight fast enough or that they are crying with hunger. 'I breast-fed Richard until he was well over two years old, because we both enjoyed our very special time together. My mother-in-law reckons I was "kinky" and "sick" and nagged me to wean him from about three months onwards!' This woman continued to breast-feed, but had to do so secretly. 'My partner's mother disapproves of Louise being breast-fed still. (She is six months old.) When we speak on the phone she always brings the subject up. Last week I was supposed to have surgery under a general anaesthetic. She said it would be a good thing if it "dried things up". I postponed the operation.'

Targets for advice

Grandmothers who described their experiences usually insisted that they did not give advice, that they knew what it was like to be at the receiving end of unwanted advice when *they* first became mothers, and that they force themselves to be silent when they see their daughters making what they think are obvious mistakes.

The younger women, however, are often acutely conscious that they are under scrutiny and cannot meet a mother's or a partner's mother's standards. So, even when nothing is said, they often feel criticized and the silence is heavy with disapproval. Here again, it is best to bring this subject out into the open, discuss it, and for the older woman to share with the younger some of her early experiences as a mother and how she, too, felt a target for advice.

I asked women whether they actively sought advice from their mothers and mothers-in-law. By far the most frequent answer was that they did not have to, because it was freely given, though often disguised as conversation about how other women are bringing up their children – a neighbour's, someone else's in the family, a woman whom she knew as a girl at school but with whom she now has nothing in common. Very young mothers are often bombarded with advice by anxious mothers and mothers-in-law. The immediate effect is to put up a defence against it. Tracey, a teenage mother with two children, says that her mother tells her, 'My 25 month old should have been toilet trained by 18 months, should have been in her own bed by 12 months, should play with toys by herself and not need me or other children with her before she will play with them. I should not have my babies to sleep with me. They should not have dummies. They shouldn't need night-time bottles. I should use cloth nappies for both the children, though our washing machine breaks down 2 to 4 times a week.' Tracey has thought very carefully about her children's emotional needs and is a skilled and sensitive mother. She says, 'I think it is traumatic for a child to be cuddled in your tummy for nine months, then put in a bed by themselves. I feel better knowing that I can hear my children breathe and when they are babies they sleep much better in bed with me. They also can't overheat when in bed with me because when it's hot I take off a blanket and we both cool down.' She thinks dummies are comforting for both the baby and the mother and says of her older child that she is a very happy little girl who only plays with her toys when other children or an adult join in because she loves to share and interact with them. As for the nappies, small children may 'go back to nappies if their secure world is changed by new surroundings'. Clearly, Tracey knows what she is doing. Her mother should stand back and admire her daughter's achievements – and, perhaps, give her a new washing machine!

Some grandmothers quote 'expert' references, and produce books of advice by paediatricians or psychologists, in order to invest their opinions with more authority. A woman says of her mother, who is doing a social work course, 'She tells me all the research she has found about babies. I don't find any of it relevant to my child and my life.' Her mother, who is enjoying making a link between the theoretical work in her university studies and her interest in her granddaughter's development, seems unaware that this is feeding her daughter's hostility to her and that it has the contrary effect to that intended. For the daughter says, 'I try my hardest to do anything and everything the opposite of how my mother would do it.' Another grandmother is a nurse and, according to her daughter-in-law, 'attempts to force her knowledge about baby routines, sleep, feeding, child health, hygiene and nutrition.' 'She is a bit of a dum-dum,' she adds. 'She gives me the shits with her ideas!'

Hard work

A frequent cause of conflict between women and their mothers and mothers-in-law is that an older woman theorizes about child-rearing but does not get down to the practical tasks. This seems to happen more with mothers-in-law than with mothers, because mothers-in-law usually do not see it as their function to be involved in details, and often expect to be treated as guests in a daughter-in-law's home. One woman's partner's mother came to stay for ten days when the baby, Caitlin, was five weeks old. 'She'd play with her.' End of story. She told me that she 'didn't change nappies'. In the time that she stayed with me she did not even make me a cuppa, believing that I was the hostess and that 'a woman should not poach in another woman's kitchen.' I asked for help. Both Caitlin and I had colds and I had a herpes attack by the end of the week, but she'd say 'I'll just have a fag first' or 'I don't like using other people's kitchens'. I was in tears of frustration and exhaustion. One night I said she would have to take over the cooking as I couldn't settle Caitlin. She cooked for her husband, herself and Ian a meat dish, wearing rubber gloves and a distasteful look on her face, and nothing for me because I am a vegetarian. I said I would just have the veg that she was cooking – and she wouldn't cook any.' Another woman says of her own mother, 'A baby is to be cuddled and given horse rides on her knee, but if he soils a nappy, is hungry, tired or irritable, she's out the door in a flash.'

Other women are in conflict with the grandmother because she overwhelms them with her domestic and management skills. Occasionally this is a mother-in-law, 'My husband's mother scrubs my house from top to tail even if it doesn't need it.' But it is usually the woman's own mother. A woman with one-year-old twins says of her mother that 'on arriving, within seconds she would zoom around and carry out any chores not already done.' She wanted to be able to sit down and talk to her mother, but had no chance to do this because her mother saw her main contribution as cleaning and cooking. So she said, 'Look, please sit down. There are things I want to ask your advice about. I can't do it if you are whizzing around like that all the time.' Her mother came to realize that she needed to be there for her daughter at a personal level, not just as a household robot. 'Nowadays,' her daughter says, 'the most she does is drying the drip-dry dishes.' There was the same problem in the relationship between a woman who was suffering from postnatal depression and her mother who, concerned that she was not coping, took over all domestic chores, but left her daughter further depressed and feeling even more of a failure after her visit. 'Her idea of help resembles the dawn-to-dusk shift in a steelworks. Consequently there is minimal time to spend with Erin or myself. She always leaves our home in a pristine condition.' She adds, 'I feel inadequate. I feel the weight of her expectations and domestic standards. There is a gap in our relationship on this psychological level.'

Power and control

Women sometimes criticize mothers and mothers-in-law for being possessive – seeking their son's or daughter's exclusive love, or claiming a grandchild as their own. They say that they draw attention to themselves whenever the focus is on anyone else, manoeuvring to redirect it towards themselves. One woman says, 'Everything in my mother-in-law's world is somehow directly connected with power and control. She showers Daniel with gifts, to the extent that I feel she is trying to stake an investment in the baby.' Another grandmother 'woos' the baby in a similar way by always showing him off and taking photographs. 'She won't get down on the floor and play. She says things to Mark like 'Come and live with Nanny. They don't know how to look after you.' Possessive grandmothers expect frequent visits and feel hurt and rejected when they do not take place with regularity. 'If we don't visit on the weekend I get the guilt trip phone call.' That guilt trip phone call is a common experience.

Suppose that you recognize ways in which, at least occasionally, you have made mistakes in this way. What do you do about it? It makes sense to think twice before picking up the phone to ring your son or daughter. At the end of the call is your child going to be happy that you have rung, or feel loaded with obligations towards you? Ask yourself if you are conveying any harmful hidden message. How can you put a positive message in its place? It is wise not to ring until you have sorted that out in your mind. Is the call a plea for attention and love because you feel left out? Or is it an expression of genuine interest in them? Are you putting them under pressure to agree to something merely to please you? Is it clear that you acknowledge their autonomy – the right to do things their way and to make their own choices? A grandmother who takes time to consider these questions is unlikely to indulge in the guilt trip phone call.

Some grandmothers have a traditional view of the family, a son's or daughter's baby is simply another addition to it, whereas their children want independence, and are not interested in reinforcing the family tree. A woman says of her mother-in-law that 'she interprets her role in the family – wife, mother and grandmother – as bestowing upon her a certain level of status. She sees it in hierarchical terms and therefore uses her position to manipulate other, more junior, members. She is jealous of my relationship with her son and believes that her contact with the baby is a birthright rather than an earned right. I do not want Emma (the baby) involved in power games of any kind.' Another woman finds herself in conflict with her mother-in-law because her husband comes from 'a very close-knit, almost suffocating, family of six children. His parents are used to them all doing things the way the family expects, with no deviations or arguments.'

Sometimes a prospective grandmother gets so involved with preparations for a coming baby that even before the birth the parents feel that she is being possessive and seeking to take control. 'It felt that the whole preparation for our coming baby had been taken out of our hands. She had done everything.' She provided not only the nappies and baby clothing, a cot and other nursery furniture, but left cans of paint in the colours of her choosing on the doorstep for the decoration of the nursery. And she insisted that they accept some money, which the young couple thought 'the ultimate insult'. 'My husband confided that it was like the baby was his mother's son, not her grandson.' After the birth 'she monopolised the baby's time' so that the father felt 'crowded out of the relationship with his own son'. The problem of how to deal with this difficult granny dominates the couple's discussions together, and the daughter-in-law concludes that 'my husband and I view the management of his mother as a long-term commitment.' As an afterthought she adds, 'But my husband turned out a nice guy and I always wondered how she managed that, so she must have done something right!'

Violent families

In families in which there is a history of abuse and violence, grandmothers are caught in a double bind. They want to be with their daughters to help them, but this may entail exposing grandchildren to possible sexual abuse or violence from a grandfather or another male family member. To protect the children they are compelled to hold back, refuse to visit, and not invite them to stay. It can be very difficult to discuss these matters or to explain to their daughters or daughters-in-law why they are keeping their distance, especially if the abuse has been shrouded in silence, or if they have colluded in the abuse by trivializing it – collusion which has been hard to resist because they themselves have suffered sexual abuse and violence.

A woman who left home at eighteen to escape from an abusive relationship with her father describes how the birth of her son, when she was thirty, led to a resurfacing of the fears and unhappiness of her childhood. When the baby was born she prayed 'that he would always feel safe at home – and that he would always feel loved', and says she was 'overwhelmed with a desire to provide my child with the happiness and sense of safety I never had.' She wanted her mother, but felt rejected because she offered no help or support. 'I felt very isolated in the first six months. My mother has let me down very badly. It is the one time of your life when you expect your mother's support, and the pain of rejection is almost worse than childhood rejection.' They only see each other on family occasions such as birthdays, and her mother is a 'virtual stranger' to her little boy. This grandmother has endured a relationship with a violent husband for close on 50 years. Looking back on it, her daughter says, 'We lived in fear. Mum was so caught up in her own problems she never imagined we were suffering. Our house was full of anger and violence all our childhood years. I never felt safe until the day I left home.' The birth of her son led to an emotional crisis. 'Since he was born the memories of my childhood have become sharper and more painful. When I look at the fragile helplessness and total trusting of my son I become very angry at the way I was treated. The twelve years I spent coming to terms with my childhood, between leaving home and having a baby, seem to have been wasted. I am having more trouble now than I did at eighteen. I am angrier than I ever was before. It has re-opened many wounds.' She says she would never let her children stay in her parents' house but longs for her mother to come and stay with her. The mother, however, is still trapped in a violent relationship with her husband, who might either insist on coming too or refuse to let her go. The only course

of action, though it may be a painful one, is for this grandmother to be open with her daughter and to tell her frankly
why she is not coming to help. Such discussion might
heal some of the wounds that all the women in this family
have suffered and so lead to new understanding.

Finding a way to heal

It may not be until a woman is herself a mother that she
can see her mother as a person. As she begins to experience
similar emotions to those her mother experienced, the anger
she felt as a child begins to heal.

As she was talking about her relationship with her mother,
one woman said, 'A friend told me to treat her as a person
and not a mother. So I do. I get along with her a lot better
now than ever before.' Exactly the same advice applies to
daughters and daughters-in-law too. When they do, it can
be for each of them a new beginning.

But it is not only a question of conflict between mothers, mothers-in-laws and daughters. Open conflict may also
develop between a grandmother and a grandchild, especially a
teenager who is experimenting with life. Many families make
silent pacts not to discuss certain topics – sex or religion,
for instance – because everyone is aware that they lead
to explosions. Researchers who studied the interaction of
80 grandparent–grandchild dyads reported that grandparents
often said, 'We never have disagreements.' They did this by
carefully avoiding conflict.[1] A skilful grandmother knows
when to disengage.

There is a common belief, stemming from pop psychology,
that the more we talk about feelings and discover our 'inner
selves', the more we solve problems and heal relationships.
This is not necessarily so. There are times when silence is
best, when thought is better than speech, when sympathetic
listening is vastly superior to confrontation. There is an art
in not allowing yourself to be drawn into conflict – and to
go beyond this and be able to still your anger and accept
other people as they are, instead of challenging and criticizing
them, an art in *learning* from a difficult situation instead of

either refusing to acknowledge it or desperately fighting to change it.

Perfect mothers do not exist. Nor do perfect grandmothers. There can be few grandmothers who have not sometimes made mistakes. The important thing is to learn from them.

Feeling Close - Mothers, Daughters and Daughters-in-law

A grandmother does not love each grandchild in the same way. She may feel closer to one, or to one family of grandchildren, than another. There are good reasons for this. Although she makes certain that the time and attention she is willing to give are equally shared out, in her heart of hearts she feels drawn to a particular grandchild or family, usually because she has closer contact with them than with the others, and has got to know them better.

When grandmothers talk about their feelings of closeness they sometimes say that they are especially pleased when a granddaughter is born, and that it is easier to understand girls because of female shared experiences. They say that boys grow away from you as they become men, while girls come closer as they become women. It does not, of course, always happen like this. There are many women who mourn psychological distancing or outright rejection by a daughter, and others who find the life-style a daughter has chosen so different from their own that it is difficult to understand or tolerate it. But, in general, women feel a common identity with daughters and granddaughters.

It is not only in post-industrial Western culture that this is so. Though sons are valued more than daughters in many cultures in which inheritance is passed down in the male line, when I was doing fieldwork in Jamaica in the 1960s mothers often told me they valued daughters and granddaughters for much the same reasons that American and British grand-mothers seem to feel a special affinity with their daughters. In Jamaica men 'run' (escape). Women stay. Men rarely nurture. Women have understanding and compassion. It is the gender division – the gender stereotypes – with which we are familiar, and which many mothers are concerned to change through the ways in which they rear their sons and daughters. But they have most of society against them.

From birth, boy babies tend to be treated differently from

girl babies. The education of boys is constructed to train them to differentiate themselves from their mothers and from the 'female' qualities mothers represent, and prepare them to fit into a man's world. 'Big boys don't cry.' Real men hide their feelings. Boys form teams and compete aggressively on the sports field. When boys are physical they fight, whereas girls are more likely to cuddle affectionately or display themselves by dressing up in pretty clothes, or by graceful movements such as dance. Mothers describe babies as young as one day old differently according to their gender. Baby girls are delicate, while boys are strong.[1] At two days mothers smile and talk more to baby girls than to boys.[2] A famous psychological study in the seventies, the Baby X experiment, revealed that a six-month-old baby, dressed either as a boy or a girl, was treated differently according to its perceived gender. A 'girl' was handed dolls, a 'boy' a train, and women smiled more at the 'girl'. The researchers concluded, 'Mothers have begun to channel children into appropriate sex roles by the age of six months. Girls are subject to more social stimulation. Also, mothers have begun to encourage sex-appropriate patterns of play. The infant emitted essentially the same behavior for all mothers, yet their treatment of him systematically differed depending on whether he was perceived as male or female.'[3] The women in this study were not aware of the differential treatment, and believed that they treated boys and girls exactly the same.

Mothers often feel that as their sons grow up they have become strangers to them. A grandmother says, for example, that she has little relationship with her son's son, who is living with his father after divorce, 'I don't know my son well. He has very different values and he is "high-powered".' She is 'horrified by his authoritarian parenting'. Another says that she was elated on learning that she was to be a grandmother and expected to be asked to baby-sit and be fully involved in her grandchild's life. But her son never even called her to tell her the baby had been born till sixteen hours later, which made her sad. Now, although they live in the same part of the city, they do not visit her and she says she is 'not always welcome' in their home. She sees her five-year-old grandson in the grocery store and hears him ask his mother who that lady is. Many women accept this with equanimity because it seems to them part of the natural order of things that a daughter-in-law should turn towards her own mother after the birth of a child, that her son visits the other grandparents more often, and as a result she loses contact. 'It stands to reason that she feels closer to her mother,' one woman says. 'But I look forward to my daughter having a baby, because with my son's child I feel a bit out of it. There is an emotional distance between us. I feel a little envious of the closeness the other grandmother has.'

Women worry that they could lose touch with their son's children as a result of divorce, while they are confident that a daughter's children will remain their grandchildren. 'I have thought how perilous my relationship with my son's kids could be if he ever divorced and lost custody of his children,' one woman says. 'This is all dark speculation. It is just that there are greater prospects of losing the grandchildren one has by a son than by a daughter.'

Intense conflict can develop in the triangular relationship between a man, a woman and his mother, causing problems not only between the man and his mother but also in a marriage. The daughter-in-law/mother-in-law relationship, like the son-in-law/mother-in-law relationship, forms part of a commonly accepted stereotype. In-law relationships are believed to be stressful. While this is so – and it may be particularly in close-knit communities – mothers feel more affinity with a daughter's than with a daughter-in-law's children, and this is sometimes explained in terms of the awkward relationship between women and the women who have 'taken away' their sons. Sociologists and psychologists have explored the images of the 'possessive mother', the tensions that seem built into the interaction between women and their mothers-in-law, and ways in which mothers-in-law are marginalized, feel relegated to the periphery of the family and may be forced to surrender the mothering role to other women.[4] In fact, many mothers-in-law are careful to stand back because they are already warned by the stock comedy figure of the mother-in-law and the ridiculing of her role in the form of numerous jokes. As a result open battles over child-rearing develop less often between a father's mother and her daughter-in-law than between mother and daughter.

Kin-keeping

Women are the 'kin-keepers' in the family.[5] They remember birthdays and anniversaries, for instance. They are family archivists and historians; they maintain inter-personal continuity like social secretaries; they record, remember and file biographies. Like diplomats, they placate, explain, negotiate and monitor behaviour. They sustain relationships on behalf of men; they keep in touch, show that they care, soothe out difficulties and mediate when things go wrong. They do this on behalf of men even before they marry and have families. Research into female undergraduate behaviour reveals that women write to their boyfriend's parents, when the sons cannot be bothered to write themselves.[6] A daughter-in-law has responsibility to keep sweet the relationship between a man and his mother.

'We didn't want to go for Christmas, and she said we were very unreasonable . . . I was in tears and she was in tears. Because I was making excuses she said, "It's unreasonable. I am his mother. Why don't you let him come?" . . . He didn't want to . . . but I didn't actually say that he didn't want to come because I thought that would upset her.'[7]

'I began to be a mediator between Alec and his mother. He didn't see a lot of his mother and I used to pass on information and news and so on. She was beginning to ask me how he was and what he was doing and what he was eating, you know.'[8]

'I know what she feels about Gareth and I hope she realises that he actually does like her and care about her. There have been occasions when she said, 'Oh, sometimes I just don't think he cares.' and I say, 'Of course he cares, he just doesn't show it.'

Since men really rarely kin-keep, there is no one to do this for a daughter-in-law in her relationship with her partner's mother. They either work on this together or there are misunderstandings and conflicts which do not get results.[9] This is obviously happening in a tense relationship between a woman and a mother-in-law who, the younger woman says, 'is jealous, at a very deep level, of my relationship with her son, and this is made worse by the fact that she was unable as a mother to achieve closeness with him.' The two women remain locked in conflict, and the man is torn between the two.

Women tend to compare a partner's mother with their own mothers, and the way the mother-in-law handles the baby, the advice she gives, her housekeeping, cooking and religious and other beliefs may all seem alien. As a woman passes through the major life transition of becoming a mother she may feel unable to cope with conflicting values and contradictory advice. One woman said of her mother-in-law, 'She was very helpful and energetic but she never does anything properly. My Mum . . . taught me that no matter how much work there is to do any job is worth doing properly. I couldn't trust Jean to do things the way I wanted them done.' The battle over who was in control came to a head one night when she was minding the baby and 'John and I came home and she had rearranged the nursery . . . changed the furniture around, put things where I couldn't get at them, hung dopey plants everywhere. I had just got the nursery exactly as I wanted it and when I saw what she had done I burst into tears. She cried too of course, and pretended to be so surprised. Poor John didn't know what to do. then Patrick woke up and started screaming and she said, "Oh I was only trying to help and now Patty's awake," and I screamed, "Stop calling him Patty! He's not a girl and he's not a cake. He's my son."'[10] The conflict proved to be not simply about different ways of doing things, but about ownership of the baby, and turned out also to be a tussle between a grandmother who longed to be admired, needed and loved and a daughter-in-law longing to build her own nest and to feel in control of her life.

Positive relationships

A grandmother may feel her son has deserted her or be uncertain whether she can love her daughter-in-law's child as much as she does her own daughter's. One grandmother who was anxious about this says, 'After the very special feelings I had when my daughter had her babies, I began to wonder if my son's child would be special in the same way or whether I could only feel that way because of my closeness to my daughter . . . I found that I loved the baby as much as my daughter's babies, but I did not feel so responsible or so involved. In many ways this is a relief. I can be more relaxed and enjoy my contact with this baby more.' For this woman, the reduced sense of obligation, her feeling that she could simply enjoy this baby without taking on responsibility, was a definite advantage.

Yet for many women there is a more precious gain. Mothers-in-law often discover that they have a new female friend – a woman who brings the son back into a living relationship with them and with whom they experience sisterhood. This is accentuated with the birth of a baby. When beforehand a woman had felt alienated from her son, now the family is once again a going concern and a mother discovers new aspects of her son's personality as he learns to be a father.

The adage 'You are not losing a son, but gaining a daughter' that is a standard part of the wedding speech, is only partly true. The older woman often finds that her son's wife relates to her woman-to-woman and that, far from being like mother and daughter, they are really more like sisters. A woman says, 'The love of one's children, at least for me, is passionate and primitive. The love for one's daughter-in-law, if one is lucky, is much more civilized, the affection one feels for a dear, younger friend.'[11] This close relationship may continue after a marriage has ended, and the link may even be strengthened by sharing child care. A woman says of her exdaughter-in-law, 'I still love her. I think she and my son are doing a great job of raising Michelle. This child is brought up with discipline and a lot of love. Because Mommy has to work, I have her two whole days a week. Her other grandmother has her two days a week, too.'

Age often divides women, and young women find it difficult to identify with those who are ageing. Younger feminists are sometimes impatient of the interests, concerns and experience of older feminists. It is as if women in their twenties have invented feminism. Sisterhood is often replaced by distancing when there are marked age distinctions in women's groups.

Yet in the relationship of mother and daughter-in-law, age

is usually far less important than differences in *values*. Where women share many of the same values – about child-rearing for example – the relationship is joyous for both. Problems come when their values conflict.

Some grandmothers are very aware of an ambivalent relationship with their in-laws, which puts stresses on their relationships with the grandchildren, too. One woman says, for example, that she does not see much of her son's child because his wife 'favours her mother, and it took her children longer to get used to me'. She is able to accept this, since she believes it is inevitable. She goes on to say, 'I feel much closer to my daughter and her children because we do more things together.' When women need help – for example after the birth of a baby – they tend to seek it from their mothers rather than their mothers-in-law. Moreover, mothers *do* things to help, while mothers-in-law *give* things. Mothers are right in doing the laundering and clearing up the kitchen, while mothers-in-law are more likely to give the spin-drier or the cot.[12]

Most grandmothers who told me about their experiences say they try not to interfere and are careful to avoid offering advice. Mothers-in-law are more wary of giving advice to daughters-in-law than are mothers to daughters. When they live in the same house or street, they avoid intruding on the young couple's life. A woman whose son and his partner and child lived in the basement flat of their house said; 'I never went down there. They came up to see me. If they were in the garden I kept away.' She has maintained a very positive relationship with her daughter-in-law. Sometimes however, women hold back so much that they appear to their daughters-in-law not to be really interested or supportive.

The best relationships seem to include a mutual sharing of ideas – woman to woman rather than older woman to junior or expert to novice – and mutual discussion about changes in child-care practices over the years. The older woman reminisces about her experience as a mother, which often includes stories about her mother and mother-in-law too, and the younger tells how the experience of motherhood is for her – her problems, quandaries, hopes and fears. Times spent talking like this create a strong bond between the two women.

One result may be unstinting admiration for a woman who coped with hardship, lack of education, racial discrimination or a violent husband – admiration, too, for all the hard work entailed in raising a family before the invention of labour-saving machines, disposable nappies, and before many husbands were motivated to share in child care and get to know their children as friends, in greater intimacy than fathers usually did 30 or 40 years before.

A woman who is finding motherhood hard going says of her mother-in-law; 'I think she is incredible to maintain sanity after 11 kids!' Another, whose relationship with her own mother is poor, lives 20 minutes' walk away from her partner's mother and says of her, 'She comes shopping with me and the children, takes the baby once a week, helps with housework when I ask, gives good advice and supports my decisions. The children love her and constantly ask to go to Nanna's house. I ask her advice about everything – the children, her son, contraceptives, and the world.'

Another, whose own home was unhappy and violent, describes her mother-in-law as 'a strong, intelligent, independent and supportive woman. I respect her immensely. She would never interfere in our lives, but would give any help if we asked. She is great! We laugh about changing theories on child care.' She concludes by saying, 'Her house is relaxed, warm and happy – a true paradise.' A woman whose mother died when she was 22 says, 'My mother-in-law has become the next best thing to a mother, and the children have brought us closer together. I was shy about getting in touch with her before the boys came along. One of the first things we had in common was infertility. It took five years to conceive our first child, and she had a two-year wait for her second, so she was one of the few people with whom I could talk frankly about my feelings . . . Gran is reluctant to push her advice because she is conscious of how things have changed, and has the wisdom not to be dogmatic. I think it still hurts her that some things she was taught to do by the great "experts" were counter-intuitive.'

When a woman misses her own mother or comes from a background in which she was deprived of love, a supportive mother-in-law can do a great deal, not only to fill the gap in her life, but to increase her self-confidence as a mother and enhance her self-esteem as a woman. Women with young children are often uncertain whether they are good enough mothers and are plagued by self-doubts; many believe that they are failures. Anything that a mother-in-law says that can communicate to her daughter-in-law that she is doing a good job, and acknowledges that the children are happy and healthy, gives her fresh courage and energy in the difficult task of mothering.

A wise grandmother never compares one son's or daughter's partner or children with others in the family. She accepts them for who they are and refuses to discuss anyone disparagingly. It may be tempting to admire one daughter-in-law's mothering skills, the support she gives her husband, her hard work, or the way she runs her home. While you acknowledge these things, never use them as an occasion to criticize, even by implication, another's character or achievement.

When Helen found that she was pregnant by her boy-friend, his mother urged him to offer her money for an abortion, as she did not think she was good enough for her son. The couple decided to have the baby, but the older woman still, whenever she could get Helen alone, 'went on and on at me to have an abortion. She thought I was common.' They got married and had the baby. But ever since then Peggy, the mother-in-law, has been comparing Helen with her other daughter-in-law, who helps her husband in a very successful business, has polite and well-turned-out children who attend an élite school, and a stylish house that she keeps immaculate. Helen, with three children born in quick succession, has suffered severe postnatal depression and feels a frump. She has a part-time job, and though she struggles to keep things clean and tidy, admits her house is a mess. The children are at state schools and are continually criticized by her mother-in-law for slovenly speech and lack of 'polish'. She offered to pay for them to go to public schools, but Helen and her husband resent this, believe in state education, and want to manage their own lives. 'She's a manipulative woman,' Helen says, 'and does her best to destroy my marriage and the relationship I have with my children.' But the children like her, 'The kids love anyone who gives them twenty quid every time they visit. She has subtle little ways of making me appear stupid in front of them, but they ignore it.'

From her mother-in-law's point of view, Helen is a disaster. 'She only works part-time. How she fills the rest of her time I don't know – her house is quite filthy,' Peggy says. 'I offered to help pay for private schools for the grandchildren. I knew that there was no way that they were going to be able to afford it on Roger's salary. All three children went to comprehensive school and there was just no need for it at all; I was quite happy to help. Angela and Jeff have sent their two children to public school and you can already see the difference.' Everything that Peggy says is fuelling the flames between her and her daughter-in-law, and now Helen has written to say that she wants to cut off all contact with her because 'You have consistently tried to sabotage my relationship with my husband and my children.' Each woman feels a victim of the other.[13]

It does not have to be like that. Even when the relationship between a woman and her partner's mother gets off to a shaky start, a mother-in-law often gets a second chance with the birth of children. At last they have an opportunity to communicate in a mutually supportive way. 'I didn't realize just how much we had in common until after Michael was born. It has strengthened our relationship immensely,' one woman says. Another tells me, 'Our relationship has changed. I feel more comfortable with her now. Sometimes I found it awkward being alone with her, but now we tend to talk mainly about the kids.' A woman who lives only 15 minutes' away from her mother-in-law says, 'I respect her more and appreciate her a lot more, and we see each other very regularly. She helps me enormously. She baby-sits the children four to five times a week and always welcomes them with open arms. She cooks dinner for us once a week, and would not hesitate to help us financially if we ever needed it. She would do anything she could to help us. She is an extended part of our family and the children see her as a second mum. I would love to do as good a job as she's done with her children. I think her ideas about children are terrific. She respects them as individual people and doesn't talk down to them.'

Happy families

Parents and grandparents extend a huge amount of energy on playing happy families. You may feel that when bad things happen in your family you do not want friends to know because you are ashamed or deeply hurt, and may have a sense of competing with peers to show that everything is fine. And when you are going through private agony your suffering may be too raw to be able to share it. Pride, or a wish to protect vulnerable family members, may prevent you from being open about an ordeal you are facing. You struggle to bear the pain alone.

But by their very nature families breed crisis. They are like pressure cookers in which emotions come to the boil, relationships steam up, and sometimes there are explosions. The 'normal' families in children's school reading schemes – Janet and John, Peter and Jane – do not exist, or if they do it is only for brief snatches of time. The joy of family life is mixed with suffering which can be some of the most acute that any human being has to bear.

The women who told me about their experiences did not only talk about the fun, excitement and other positive aspects of being grandmothers – they also talked about the pain. Sharing pain may be just as important as sharing joy, if we are to grow in understanding. Grandmothers, of all people, should see family life from a perspective which enables them to accept reality and be honest about it. Otherwise we simply perpetuate a fantasy – the fantasy of a family that is always happy.

In my work as an antenatal teacher I learned about the pain that many couples experience as they approached parenthood; I talked with men and women about not only the pleasures of expecting a baby, but about darker thoughts and feelings too. The standard happy pregnant couple is a construct of wishful thinking. Many couples were facing emotional challenges, and the path to parenthood was far from easy. To limit the classes to solely the teaching of how to breathe and relax would have been to deceive the parents-to-be, and for some would have been totally irrelevant anyway. So I began to teach workshops for antenatal teachers to explore emotional themes. One startled teacher said to me, 'I can't make it out, Sheila. I can't understand why you get such peculiar women in your classes. All my gals are normal!'

We often act as if all families were 'normal', imposing a stereotype of normality on what is actually a complicated reality. When we do this we prevent ourselves from being able to accept and deal with deviations from this artificial 'norm'.

Stormy relationships

A grandmother may be unaware that she is stimulating sibling rivalry and even exploiting it for her own ends, when she talks about her children, their partners and their children, and compares or contrasts personal appearance, behaviour, possessions, styles of parenting or achievements. Even if she does not do this deliberately, siblings who are already competitive may take casual remarks as criticism, 'She thinks Lynn's kids have better manners than ours. She's always going on about it', 'When she came to stay she commented on how often Oliver wakes for a feed. She says David is going through the night already', 'She boasts about Dawn's children and how well they are doing at school. I'm sick of hearing about it. My kids are OK!'

When a woman pays attention and devotes a lot of time to a daughter who has made her a grandmother, other sisters may feel left out in the cold. We have seen already that a mother and daughter often draw closer together after the birth of a baby. The mother relives lovingly remembered significant experiences in her own life as her daughter passes through pregnancy, birth and motherhood. The conflicts typical of adolescence are often swept aside as interests are shared. The baby provides a bridge of communication and the older woman revels in a new closensess with this special daughter.

In fact, it may not be such an intimate relationship as the grandmother believes, for as we saw in Chapter 6 the younger woman may feel the strain of her mother's enthusiasm for babies and baby things. But the new grandmother who exults in what she sees as a new intimacy may hold this daughter up as a shining example of womanliness, and compare her favourably with another, who is committed to her career and has decided not to have a baby, who has not found the right man, whose marriage has broken up, who is lesbian, or who cannot get pregnant or hold on to a pregnancy. Sometimes the non-mother is turned into an outcast. She has let the family down. Whatever her other achievements, she is a failure in her mother's eyes.

Even previously 'happy families', in which members generally like each other, are then shattered. Phone calls and letters become the ammunition in an internecine war, family get-togethers are like time bombs. The baby is sure to cry. Older children are bound to 'act up'. There is weeping behind locked bathroom doors, pillow talk in which couples recount the horrors of each day, and whispered conversations that are broken off when someone opens the door.

The dysfunctional family is not only a family where there is violence and sexual abuse. It can be *any* family which disintegrates under emotional demands made on it by a mother or father for whom 'love' is in reality 'control', and in which the members are played off against each other in the effort to manipulate them more effectively.

You may feel sure that you would never behave like that. Or when you stand back you may see that there are times when your emotional needs were so great that you have exploited others in this way. You may also remember how, as a young woman yourself, battles like this were fought in your own or in a close friend's family. Awareness can bring understanding of often apparently irrational behaviour, of the seething emotions that come to the boil under the lid of family life, that explode in disputes, and drive family members to escape from each other.

A Learning
Experience

B eing a grandmother is, above all, a learning experience. One woman sums this up, 'I have become a complete human being, able to love and freely love and nurture small human beings. They have, in many ways, made me know myself much better. I am contented, fulfilled, confident. They have shown me how to *love unconditionally.'*

When you reflect on everything that you are discovering about yourself and other people, and about the values important to you, there can be no doubt that becoming a grandmother gives you an opportunity for personal growth and developing greater understanding. Some women resist this opportunity because change is too painful for them. Other seize it and gain a new zest in life from doing so.

Culture shock

For some women, coming face to face with a daughter's very different views of parenting results in confrontation. 'I have learned,' one woman comments sadly, 'how much my daughter thinks I went wrong in bringing her up.' It is hard to look back at how you were as a mother and admit that you made mistakes. But, of course, we all have – just as our daughters and daughters-in-law will also make mistakes, though they may be different ones. It can be hard, too, for a daughter to acknowledge the pressures that you were under as a mother in a social situation which was very different from hers. Perhaps you had less money. Certainly you had fewer labour-saving devices, such as a washing machine, a dishwasher and drier, and disposable nappies may not have been invented. You may have reared your children at a time when it was accepted that men contributed to parenthood by having a job and giving their financial support, but did not need to be emotionally involved or offer much practical help in other ways. The conditions in which you mothered may have allowed only limited choices so that you were less relaxed about discipline, for example, than your daughter is with her child. You may have had bad advice about infant feeding, were told that feeds should be given only every four hours, so the baby did not gain weight, your breasts became engorged, your nipples got sore, and you may have suffered from mastitis or a breast abscess, and as a result gave up breast-feeding. Perhaps you did not cuddle your baby as much as she does because you were taught that babies should be put down and needed undisturbed sleep. Maybe your priorities were cooking and cleaning, rather than spending time with your child, partly because, in the conditions of those days, the practical tasks of running a home were a full-time job in themselves, and because you were under pressure from others, including parents and parents-in-law, to have everything clean and tidy, meals ready on time, and the children well-turned out and well-behaved.

Talking about this with your daughter or daughter-in-law, you begin to understand the other better. One consequence of such discussion is that you probably change your priorities and practices. Many grandmothers say that their beliefs about child-rearing have altered radically. 'I swatted my kids,' one grandmother says. 'Now I have learned to discipline without hitting.' Another, 'I have learned to be more patient. My daughter is an inspiration.' A grandmother notices that she has far more patience with her grandchild than she had with her own children, 'It is not important that jobs don't get done. When he toddles to me with a book I sit on the floor and read to him. I build with his bricks. I play "peep" – I sing to him. I dance with him (Tina Turner has nothing on me!), I chase him, I laugh with him. I do all these things with him that I never seemed to find time to do with my own. I guess I was so busy trying to make my own kids perfect, I never found the right balance to enjoy them and savour every stage of their development.'

You can still have your ways of doing things which are different from your daughter's or daughter-in-law's. If you know that when children come to stay it will irritate you to have them around till late at night, if you worry about small hands exploring a cupboard where precious cut glass or china is kept or, much more frightening, the cupboard under the sink with its bottles of bleach, drain cleaner and other poisonous substances, make some firm, simple rules. If you dislike them tramping straight in from the garden in muddy shoes onto a white carpet, if you cannot stand children eating on the hoof and scattering crumbs all over the house, set boundaries – and do it at the outset! Keep them to the minimum and be absolutely clear about them!

Under two year olds are unlikely to cope with rules that are very different from those at home unless they are part of a family group all doing the same thing. But once past that age children can acknowledge that people want different things and that they should adapt their behaviour. Explain, for instance, that the custom in your house is just like in Japan: all outdoor shoes are left at the door and you have special slippers for them to wear. If constructional toys lie in drifts in doorways and on stairs in their own home, show them the decorated toy box that will keep all their bits and pieces safe and the exhibition shelves where they can display their models. Plan special before-bedtime treats: a bubble bath, singing together, looking at a family photograph album and talking about what Mummy or Daddy did when they were children, a story cassette to which a child can listen with headphones, *only* to be used in bed, while you have your evening meal. Build a happy bedtime ritual so that the child looks forward to it, and never rush it!

A grandmother who says that she was brought up 'according to the draconian regime of Dr Truby King with four-hourly feeds and eight-hour nights', and who turned to Dr Spock for guidance with her own children, obviously thinks that her daughter is sacrificing herself to her children, for she is 'entirely yielding, tender and indulgent'. Her solution when small grandchildren come to stay is to tell them firmly that her rules are different from their Mummy's. She explained that 'they would have a nice supper, a nice bath, a nice long story and a nice kiss, and not a sound did I want to hear once they had been settled in bed. Astonishingly, it worked. Nor do they dread coming to stay. They recognise that funny old Granny has different rules and you might as well obey them.'[1] If she has been able to do this *without criticizing her daughter* the strategy has worked well. If there is even implied criticism of how her daughter rears her children the two of them need to talk and come to understand and accept their differences.

There have been huge changes in expert advice about what children should eat over the last 20 or 30 years too, while at the same time the range of processed fast food and junk foods that children gobble, and which are advertised before and after children's television programmes, has spread widely. Mothers today want their children to have healthier diets, and need your support in this. You may have allowed your own child sweets as treats and awards for good behaviour. If he sat still while you removed the splinter in his hand he could have some Smarties. Your daughter or daughter-in-law may try to stop her child, especially the first-born, from having sugar, and when you protest 'One chocolate can't do any harm' or 'Only once a week!' she gets upset. Current dietary advice is that sugary, high-fat and salty foods should be only a small proportion of a child's diet. When sweet foods are eaten they should form part of a meal and be followed by a drink of water. A wise grandmother uses her imagination to think up other foods that contain natural sugars: a banana, for instance, some grapes, nectarines or satsumas. Grandmothers who resist the urge to turn up with packets of chocolate biscuits and to give children sugary drinks, ice cream and sticky lollipops or toffees when they are 'good', help build healthy eating habits, which not only save children from toothache and painful visits to the dentist, but can also have a positive effect on their health as adults.

Many mothers today read about child nutrition and worry about the junk food habit. This is why conflicts between mothers and daughters are often about what a child eats, and when women criticize their mothers it is because when they give treats they do so in the form of food – especially sweets – or are not aware that many products contain additives and colourings to which the children are allergic or which make them hyperactive. Some say that they cannot trust their mothers to baby-sit for this reason, or that they cross-question their children after visits, knowing that granny will have slipped them something they are not allowed and that their pockets are bulging with toffees.

So if you want to avoid conflict, find out which foods are acceptable treats. Maybe fruit can take the place of Smarties and ice lollies. Flapjacks baked without dairy products may suit a child better than the cakes you usually make. Some young children cannot tolerate wheat, so ground rice is a better cereal to use.

A grandmother may think nothing of smoking in front of the children. Perhaps she has always smoked and thinks that it is too late to change her ways. The children's parents may disapprove strongly, but withhold criticism or soft-pedal complaints, because they realize that she finds it hard to kick the habit. However, not only is it harmful for pregnant women and children to be in smoky rooms, but when a loved grandparent smokes it implies that this is an acceptable activity, and one which is a symbol of being grown-up. If you do not want to stop smoking, think how you can modify your behaviour so that you never smoke in the presence of your grandchildren. The birth of a grandchild sometimes provides sufficient incentive for a woman to cut out smoking entirely, and her own health improves as a result.

But smoking is only one issue. Your children may be acutely conscious of risks to their children which never occurred to you. A mother who is a journalist writes of a 'house of horrors' – 'this "death trap" which is Grandma and Grandpa's house' – and is astonished that she herself survived childhood.[2] The present generation of parents is targeted with warnings about dangers of which the grandparents' generation was blissfully oblivious: the risk of botulism from giving honey to babies, salmonella from raw or soft-boiled eggs, listeria from soft cheese, the dangers of spending a day beside the sea in bright sunshine and getting a lovely tan but increasing the risk of later skin cancer, having bottles of pills around without child-proof caps, keeping poisonous cleaning materials in the cupboard under the sink, failing to buckle each child into a safety seat before going off in the car and running the risk of a serious accident – even of leaving a child to play outside where he or she might be kidnapped or abused.

As the children grow into their teens, a grandmother becomes aware of an entirely new culture and begins to learn its language. A grandmother of four, the oldest of whom is fourteen, says she now knows about 'Doc Martens and Reeboks and shell suits and other generation interests like computer games and skateboards'. The children watch too much TV, do not obey their parents, and argue about what they are going to do and when they are going to do it. In fact, their family life may seem to you chaotic. But if you learn to be silent and to keep an open mind, as you watch, you will begin to understand more. As we get older it is not only muscles that seize up. We risk losing our mental agility and becoming narrow-minded and dogmatic.

If you are authoritarian, locked into prejudices and unwilling to learn, grandmothering is bound to be painful. You need the grace to accept what cannot be altered, the flexibility to adapt to change, and the generosity and warmth to give your children and grandchildren unconditional love.

The grandmother as student

The idea that older people are wiser than younger ones simply because they have been around longer went out with the advent of the age of electronic information. In a book for grandparents, a couple who have devised a special 'curriculum' to help heal intergenerational conflicts state, 'Older people are no longer regarded as experts about much of anything except aging.'[3] Instead of knowledge being handed *down*, it is communicated *across*. In many ways it always was, of course. Children acquire information (or misinformation) behind bicycle sheds, on street corners, talking earnestly behind the closed doors of bedrooms, or in huddled groups in the playground. Children's rhymes and games are a treasure store of information and attitudes to politics, sex and society communicated between children. In the process children distort, ridicule and lampoon, criticize or condemn the culture in which they live and the behaviour of adults.

Television has added another, sometimes more accurate, but often more confusing, dimension. It can be difficult to separate reality from fiction, opinion from fact. Where do the news and documentaries end and soap and *Star Wars* begin? If it is hard for adults, it is especially problematic for young children to work out.

When you become a grandmother you often find yourself making cross-references between your grandchildren's lives – how they learn, what they do, and the way in which their parents are bringing them up – and the memories you have of your own children's lives and how things were for you as a child yourself. You worry that your grandchildren are watching too many TV and video programmes and are playing violent computer games when they should be out climbing trees, learning the three Rs or playing chess. It may be difficult to accept the electronic culture which your grandchildren consider normal.

If you are to begin to understand the world in which they are living you have to acknowledge the electronic revolution that has taken place. You need to know how to tap sources of information other than memory or the encyclopaedias on the bottom shelf, and check your knowledge against these new sources of information. When you learn how to use the technology, even if your performance remains at a basic level, you can help your grandchildren acquire the skills of analysis and criticism as they absorb this information too. For electronic information depends on the accuracy of the human beings who fed the data into the programme.

Watch what your grandchildren watch on TV and video. All ways of providing information also communicate *values*. There is no way that even the most scientific and factual of programmes does not embody the values of the programme makers and present their view of the world.

Most computer games are sexist and violent, based on male fantasies of domination, capture, killing and extermination. Women are the prizes, victims or accessories. A 1991 study of Nintendo games showed that of 47 leading games only 7 did not involve violence.[4] Sam, nearly seven, watches videos and plays computer games, and when I put this to my daughter, Tess, she protests, 'But what about comics? They are aimed at the same age group!' Jon, her husband, buys him the *Beano*, 'At least the computer games develop the child's logic.'

This is how conversation went:

Me I can see that a child has to think through different strategies, and that these computer games are educational in that sense.

Tess For reading, too. Children of, say, four to seven, learn to read when they play these games. With comics you don't really need to read, the pictures tell the story. With many computer games you have to read instructions or else you can't play. For five to seven year olds videos help develop reading skills.

They present problems to be solved, and at an earlier age hand–eye co-ordination.

Me But it's awful to see children stuck in front of a machine, not talking, not communicating, not sharing with other children.

Tess The boys talk about the programmes. And there are some games that encourage discussion between parents, or for that matter between grandparents and children. They are targeted at, say, five year olds and offer multiple-choice questions such as, 'Shall we go to the seaside today?' You sit down and play this with the children and talk about the options.

Me Videos and TV are more often used as child-minders just to keep children quiet and out of the way. That's what worries me.

Tess Boys long to be part of a gang. They play the same videos and talk about them together and feel they are one of the gang. That is important for a seven year old. The other boys have the video, so he wants it too.

Me You're saying that they offer security and social acceptance with their peers, because kids can discuss them, and that this also stimulates communication?

Tess Yes. But now that Sam can read well, he actually often prefers books. And if I offer to read him a story – not just after he's switched on or when he is engrossed in a game – but at the right time, when he is a bit bored or not really involved in it, he always chooses the story.

That conversation resulted in my deciding that if I am to compete with video games and TV I must offer exciting, real-life alternatives and engage his interest in things to make and do. If I do not have the energy to do this all the time, what is the point of criticizing? It is up to me to make alternative activities more attractive to him.

As we talked I remembered that video games which are all

about the enemy are not all that different from the comics of my own childhood. I did not read them much, but my younger brother had piles of them. They were page after page of 'bang! thug! grrrr . . . ! squelch!' and stories of the triumph of the boy wonder over his competitors. My mother was as appalled by my seven-year-old brother's reading material as I am by my grandson's computer games. My brother later became a pacifist and conscientious objector, though he retained his fascination with the media and later still became a TV producer and, among other things, was editor of the TV programme *Panorama*. Comics may have had a formative influence in his life, but not in the way Mother expected!

So hold back on criticism. Observe and ask questions. That way you start to learn about your grandchildren's world. TV programmes can be a good source of discussion with children. You might start with advertisements. They have probably seen them dozens of times, so you can talk over them without being told to shut up. Deconstructing advertisements can help a child develop critical faculties. But avoid making heavy weather of it. Keep a light touch, 'Do you think this is really true? Is there anything that probably *isn't* true? What are they trying to make us think? How do they want us to *feel*?' Analysis has to be fairly simple for six to eight year olds, but even at that age children can be surprisingly astute. They may find it fun to construct their own advertisements – for something they have made themselves, for instance.

As you continue to watch programmes together, ask more questions. During intervals and just after a programme has finished, discuss what happened. Television offers many opportunities to explore the issues of right and wrong, 'What would *you* have done? What do you think happens next? Should he have done that? If you were her friend, how do you think you could help her? Who was the best person in that film? Was that one *really* bad? Do you think that was the right thing to do? Why did he do it? What should he have done instead? How do you want that story to end? Which parts of that programme do you think were best?' You can talk about frightening things too, 'That was *scary*!' The child is then helped to disclose his own fears, if he wants to, in a safe and accepting relationship where he knows he will be understood because you, too, get frightened. Situations in TV and video stimulate other discussions of that kind, too – about loneliness, fear, bullying, being lost, encountering death, and about war and violence.

Do not lay down the law. Explore the issues that are raised. Enable the child to express thoughts without imposing your own opinions. Be gentle. Have fun!

Once you do this, you may be ready to plunge into cyberspace and virtual reality.

Crisis management – crisis watching

Parenthood is a perilous enterprise. It is always fraught with uncertainty. By the time you are a grandmother you know that the potential for tragedy is there, as well as for fulfilment. A *New York Times* columnist, Anna Quindlen, writes about how as a child she watched birds who had lost their chicks, and once found baby rabbits beneath the stiffening corpse of their mother. She tried to rear them, but one by one they died, 'Now I know that much of parenthood is watching and waiting for the chick to fall into harm's way, watching and waiting for the cats and the cold nights. The joyous enterprise has an undercurrent of terror . . . It is the randomness of it that is so awful . . . Children step in front of cars and fall in pools; teenagers take the wrong drugs, drive too fast, dip too deep into some well of despair . . . Some grow up strong with bad upbringings, and some falter with good ones.'[5]

When there is a crisis in the family, a grandmother often finds herself at the hub of it. A child is desperately ill, a daughter dies, a father abuses a child, a couple split up, a grandchild gets in trouble with the law. She wants to rescue them from disaster, sort out financial problems, offer a refuge for a grandchild who has been thrown out or has run away from home. She sees dramas unfolding, suffering inflicted. Sometimes she aches to help, but cannot. One very important thing the grandmother can give, in the words of one who has learned to ride the storms of family life, is 'calm, love and fun in the midst of chaos'. She hears her children's and grandchildren's pain and anger, but does not allow herself to be overwhelmed by it. She learns how to be an expert in crisis management, even when she seems to be giving no more than understanding sympathy.

Some grandmothers see their grandchildren only once a year, or on family celebrations that are carefully scripted and managed to avoid confrontation and unpleasantness. They may escape these particular challenges. Others are right in there, giving twenty-four-hour care. When this happens, there is a blurring of the edges between mothering and grandmothering.

We have seen already that in the Caribbean, for example, grandmothers are often rearing two broods, their own and their daughters' children, and see themselves, and are seen by the children, as mothers rather than grannies. This is how it often used to happen in England, too, among working-class families. A midwife who worked in the pit villages around Barnsley in Yorkshire in the 1920s recalls, 'The babies were just sort of absorbed into the family . . . The grandmother became the mother in most cases . . . She would look after the baby and the girl would go back to work – in the mills or domestic work.'[6]

This is also how it often is today when families have disintegrated or a mother is unable to mother. One in every five American children is a member of a reconstituted family following divorce. These children have often been caught up in the acrimony as a marriage turned sour, relationships deteriorated, and open conflict – sometimes involving physical violence – resulted. They have experienced confusion, emotional turmoil and divided loyalties. A grandmother watches helplessly as the relationship breaks up. She tries to make up for the dreadful mistakes that her own children have made. She sees the children stressed, often treated as possessions or pawns in a bitter game, with disputes over their custody. She is acutely aware that separation or divorce may take her grandchildren from her. She trains herself to be silent, and above all never to criticize, lest she lose them. Some grandmothers resist all emotional involvement with their grandchildren in case they have to lose them, either because they move to another city or country, or as the result of divorce. Grandparents have, as a rule, no rights. Nor do children have the right to continue a relationship with loved grandparents after their parents' marriages have broken up. Grandmothers take on mammoth tasks to keep families together, and to give grandchildren a home. In the United States, however, grandparents who obtain legal guardianship of their grandchildren are not eligible for financial and other assistance which official foster parents get.

Grandmothers are unsung heroines. Louise, for example, has five sons, two biological grandchildren, and a clutch of step-grandchildren whom she has never met. The daughter-in-law who is the mother of the grandchildren is drug dependent, was abused as a child and has severe emotional difficulties. Louise looks after these children as 'more of a parent than a grandparent'. She says, 'I must be their mother.' Her son's wife had the first baby when she was seventeen and unmarried. 'I was afraid she might opt for abortion or adoption and that my son might reject her. I feared losing my grandchild.' The second baby had to remain in hospital following birth because of the drugs she had received from her mother's bloodstream, and was released into her grandmother's care after a visit by a social worker. Louise has learned to be the still, stable centre of a family in which there is a great deal of pain and distress. She has come out of it a stronger woman, enriched in the process.

Women bring to grandmothering a surprising exuberance and enthusiasm. 'I feel that I have learned more with and from my seven-year-old granddaughter than I did from my four children, because her Mom wasn't around and I stepped in,' one woman says. She became so involved that, together with parents of other children, she started a playgroup which developed into a kindergarten. After her daughter had returned to work when the baby was six months old, a woman decided to retire and move 3000 miles to care for her granddaughter, now nearly two years old. It is a more than full-time job, demanding her commitment right through the week, and often through weekends as well. She herself was the mother of twins and, in contrast, she says that 'one at a time is wonderful. I have the joy of watching the flower unfold.' For many grandmothers it is as if their eyes have been opened to a child's development for the very first time. Some say that when they were mothers they were far too busy to stand back and watch. Yet this cannot be a sufficient explanation, for grandmothers who are giving full-time mothering have often learned how to do this too. Perhaps the difference is that when a woman is a mother, particularly for the first time, her perception of a child tends to be infused with anxiety. By the time she is a grandmother most of that anxiety has disappeared, and she can enjoy each moment and each phase of the child's development as it comes.

On the other hand, anxiety based on experience and understanding has a function. It prepared one woman, whose own son had died in childhood, for accepting that her baby grandson is almost completely blind. She spent agonizing weeks after his birth on guard against worrying her daughter unnecessarily. 'This child never looked at anyone. He did smile, but there was no eye-to-eye contact. My daughter kept asking me, "When will he smile, Mum?" "Won't be long now, another few days," I would cheerfully reply, while my heart grew heavier with the awful realisation that all was not well. Eventually I had to tell her my fears.' After tests revealed that he was blind in one eye and had little sight in the other she was 'overjoyed' because she had convinced herself that he was autistic. Her husband was relieved, too, because he works with special needs children and had worried that the child was brain-damaged. She is suffused with love for this child, and the pain she has experienced from the death of her own son is being healed in the process.

Yet things may be happening in a family, crises encountered and pain suffered, of which a grandmother has only a slight inkling. She may suspect that something is wrong but cannot pin-point it. Or she may hide from herself an agonizing reality, recognition of which would mean that she would be completely unable to cope. So she protects herself by not seeing it. One woman has her grandchildren, aged fourteen and four, to spend every evening with her, and delights in this. She rolls on the lawn with the younger one, plays pretend in the sand-box, reads stories, pushes him in the swing, and sings songs. She makes clothes for them and writes short stories about her own childhood. She plays games with her fourteen-year-old granddaughter, helps with homework, reads the books her granddaughter recommends and discusses them with her, and lets the teenager borrow her grandmother's sweatshirts and T-shirts. At first her description sounded like an almost ideal family with an ideal granny. But she went on to say that their father is an alcoholic and abusive and violent. He is having therapy, but lives in a trailer just outside the family's house, free to wander in and out. The fourteen year old hates her father, refuses to speak to him or be in the house at the same time as him, and is having counselling. The children are with their grandmother every evening because their mother is working and they have to be protected from their father. Though the grandmother provided all this information, she does not seem fully aware of the long-term emotional effects of such abuse on the teenage girl. When her granddaughter says how much she hates her father she admonishes her and tells her that she 'ought to be more forgiving'.

Recognizing sexual abuse in the family may entail admitting that a grandmother's partner has abused his children or grandchildren. A woman who had been repeatedly raped by her father relived this, in all its pain and violence, during a difficult birth in which she was denied any control over what was being done to her. Her mother was either completely unaware that her husband had abused their daughter, or could not acknowledge it because it was too painful. 'I've thought about telling Mum about the abuse. Perhaps I'll be able to do it. But it's hit me that she did absolutely nothing to stop it,' the daughter says. 'He used to bathe me until I started getting pubic hair. He used to touch me in the bath. I keep getting flashes from the past. Dad is carrying me upstairs. He kept a washing line on the landing with which to tie me up. I feel hot and frightened. He got pleasure out of making me cry.' She is now deeply depressed, has suicidal urges and says of her three-year-old, 'Why should she be happy? I think about killing her.' The grandmother resists facing up to what has happened, and now the grandchildren are also in danger.

In other families it is very different. Diane and her sister were abused by their father. Diane now has two young children and was at her parents' house at a family gathering with them when her father took the little boy and his cousin out in his car without asking her whether this was all right. Her grandmother immediately picked up on her distress. 'My Nan was really furious. She said, "If he lays a finger on that boy I'll kill him." My Nan saved us from him so many times. I used to spend weekends with her, mainly to avoid going home.'[7]

A mother may go to great lengths to shield her own mother from the knowledge that a grandchild has been sexually abused because she feels ashamed that she could not protect her child.

Kathy's daughter, Rose, was abused by her second husband, the child's stepfather. She has now divorced him. Her parents have loved and supported her whatever happened in her life. They are born-again Christians with strong moral principles and are very opposed to divorce. 'I feel tainted and Rose feels ten times worse than me,' says Kathy. She has told them about the abuse. 'It hurt me. God knows, it hurt Rose. But how it must have hurt them! But they've been tolerant and done everything they can to help.'[8] This grandmother responded in a caring and compassionate way. There are others who do not really hear what is being said, pretend they have not been told or angrily deny that it could possibly have happened. When grandmothers close their eyes to child sexual abuse it may be because it is too shocking to admit, because they feel helpless to do anything about it, or because they themselves are abused.

Loss of control

It is important to accept the partners your children choose, though they may be very different from those you would have selected yourself. This is often difficult. If you doubt whether a relationship will last you are bound to feel anxious when a daughter gets pregnant, because *you* know, though she may not, that babies do not mend marriages, but bring extra stress. One grandmother worried as a relationship went from bad to worse and her daughter, trying to patch up the marriage, produced two babies. She left her husband when the children were two and three years old and came to live with her mother, who resents the child-centred life that has been forced upon her and at the same time feels out of control of everything that happens. She explains the problems in terms of her own personality, and apologizes for how she feels. She says, 'The urge to protect my daughter, my need always to intervene and support, is exhausting me.' She thinks that somehow it must be all *her* fault.

Becoming a grandmother means surrendering control. 'The balance of power has shifted. When my children were growing up, family life often revolved around me. Partly because I was so busy, we ate when I scheduled meals; frequently we went to exhibitions, plays or films that I wanted to see, when I had time to see them; and we visited friends or relatives when they could be squeezed into my already overextended life. In the household of Janet and Jonny today, I have to work around the needs of my grandchildren and the active lives of their parents.' She sees it as being 'dethroned'.[9] Even the name a child is given may grate on your ears. One grandmother wrote to Ann Landers, appalled that her son and daughter-in-law intended to christen their baby daughter 'McDuff' – the mother's maiden name. The granny said she was 'insulted'. Landers told her it was nothing to do with her and advised her to keep quiet.

It is difficult for a woman to accept that it is no longer her show when she was been landed with all the problems but allowed to exert no influence over the situations into which younger members of the family drift or are pushed by adverse circumstances. A grandmother who sets great store on management may feel panic when she witnesses children behaving badly and beyond parental control. One bitter and resentful grandmother who talked to me about her son's children said, for example, 'His wife is not in control of the children and it drives me crazy.' She also criticized another family of grandchildren for their rudeness, 'They've learned how to treat me from watching and listening to their father, and while I take it from him, I can't from them.' A six-year-old grandson is 'too thin', 'catches everything' and is allergic to bee stings. Her daughter-in-law, however, '*asks* him if he will wear the Medic Alert bracelet and sighs when he refuses'. She comments, 'I expected my children to remember their training and to use it on their children, and I am so disappointed that they don't.' When she tries to discipline them she complains that she almost gets her tongue bitten off by their parents. She realizes that this is alienating her children and grandchildren. For her, being a grandmother is a depressing experience and she avoids her grandchildren as much as possible. A social worker, whose daughter's marriage broke up leaving her with children, aged two and three, now has her daughter and the children living with her. She remarks, 'I am a very controlling person.' As a mother she managed things like potty training, bedtime behaviour and what her children ate, and usually gave them no choice. But now she has to defer to a daughter who believes in democratic discussion and decision-making, even with little children. She says, 'I have learned painfully to take a back seat.' Since she has come to accept that her daughter is mothering in a different way, it is much easier for her.

This may not be so simple when a horde of grandchildren descend on you. Visiting grandchildren can sweep through a house like a tornado. You made everything ready for them, planned carefully, cleaned, cooked, arranged flowers, set out playthings, and looked forward to their coming. When they arrive they are on their best behaviour for all of ten minutes. Then hell breaks loose. The babies cry, have their nappies changed, are fed, spit up, are fed again and changed once more. The older ones shout, quarrel, fight, break things, bang doors, scream, walk on the carpet in muddy shoes, and turn the living room and kitchen into obstacle courses of toys and plastic construction sets that have never got as far as being constructed or have been threateningly deconstructed. A couple of five-to-seven-year-old boys and a clutch of toddlers soon turn into a kid mob. Sara Paretsky touches on what some grandmothers feel when she has a woman say, at the reception following her husband's funeral, 'Kerry took the children to her house, so things will be a little calmer today,' and adds, 'Maybe when I retire I'll move to Oregon.' Detective Warshawski hugs her and says, 'Go across the country to avoid being a grandmother? Maybe you could just change the locks – it'd be less drastic.'[10]

In spite of this, grandmothers often adapt with amazing grace to child-rearing practices very different from their own. A grandmother aged sixty-seven, with arthritis of her hands, feet and knees, is full-time carer of her granddaughters of four and two for three days a week, while their mother works as a midwife in another city. 'In fact they are with us five days because my daughter has to come down the day before and goes back the day after, and I get up at 4.30 am to wake Clare at 5.00 am in time to catch the 6.00 am train, and she works a twelve-hour shift and does not get home till 10.30 pm.' The children wake around 8.00 am and this grandmother has them all day until late at night. 'I try to encourage them to have a couple of hours sleep around 4.00 pm so that they can last out to see their Mum at 10.30 pm.' They are, she says, 'beautiful little girls, but very demanding in comparison to my own four children with whom I was very strict. When I told them to do something I wanted it done immediately and not when they felt in the mood to do it.' Yet she 'thanks God every day for our blessing'.

You may feel useless when a child or grandchild is in trouble or seriously ill. One grandmother who talked to me is giving full-time care to her grandchildren aged five and two because their mother is drug dependent. She shoulders full responsibility for this because her partner works very long hours. There is nothing she can do about the situation except get on with it as best she can. Women who have professional skills that ought to be relevant, and still can do nothing, feel especially that they are failing their children. Rosalind is a psychotherapist. Her daughter's baby was born with a heart defect. He was operated on when he was thirteen days old, but died. 'I recognised that there was nothing I could do to relieve my daughter's pain and distress; she had to find her own way of coming to terms with the death of her baby.'

While some grandmothers are drawn into child care when there is tragedy, many others feel marginalized. 'I am no longer at the centre of things – just someone on the sidelines who is called on to help in an emergency.' A marriage breaks up, a teenager is on drugs, a husband is violent, a daughter gets depressed, a grandchild is sexually abused, becomes emotionally disturbed or physically ill, or the children's parents let them 'run wild'. A wise grandmother watches, helps unobtrusively, and avoids dishing out unwanted advice. One woman says, 'The worst thing is seeing my grandchildren hurt, made anxious or unhappy by their parents' behaviour to them or to each other, and standing by and not interfering. I am surprised how painful this is.'

A woman who has six grandchildren says she did not expect the helplessness she feels. Both her children's marriages have broken up. Her son's wife left him and she had to take over the five-month-old baby. All the grandchildren have to cope with the trauma of accepting step-parents and disputes over custody. Grandmothering leaves her feeling frustrated and helpless: helpless when a row of children are glued to 'rubbish' on the television, when the house is bedlam, and when nothing she says or does can influence the course of events.

Even when things seem to be going well, grandmothers often

feel that time and energy is wasted in discussion and negotiation with children, who may be allowed, even encouraged, to choose what they eat, for instance. A woman who brought her children up on a farm where food choices were limited, and where meals were served and eaten without comment and as a matter of course, says, 'I tended to put food on the table and it was all eaten. There was no expectation that they were "lazy eaters". The problem was not *what* they would eat but how to fill them up.'

The sense of loss of control, like being in a car when the brakes fail, is frightening. It means that a grandmother may say or do things without thinking through possible consequences, that she lays down the law about children's behaviour, for example, or offer advice when it is not wanted, because she is anxious and feels that everything has got out of hand.

Fear reduces the quality of grandparenting. Two groups of adults were given a co-operative task to perform and told that the banging in the next room was rebuilding which had to continue because the builders were behind schedule. One group were told that nothing could be done about the noise, the other that if the noise got too bad they could instruct the workers to stop for a while. The group who had control over the noise performed significantly better than those who had no control over it.[11]

Your children's partners may not be those you would have wanted. They may be repeating mistakes that you made, their children's education and upbringing may be different from how you would have chosen. But *you* cannot make decisions for them.

Grandmothers who seek to gain control feel powerless and rejected when they are ignored, and this happens especially when there is no easy, on-going interaction with children and grandchildren, when visits are special events and there is little opportunity for casual contact. When women live far away from their grandchildren, visits can be over-organized and too much significance attached to everything that is done and said.

Sometimes a grandmother plans to move so that she can be nearer. That is not always a good idea. If you are thinking of moving house consider the pros and cons carefully and talk them through with your daughter or son and their partners. Listen to what they say and also, if you can, to what they are *not* saying but may be wanting to say. Remember how it was in your relationship with your mother and mother-in-law when you had young children, and use that understanding to guide you in coming to a decision, too.

In your central position as a grandmother it may be tempting to try to knit a family together which is drifting apart – to have, as it were, all your children around you and your grandchildren at your knee in peace and harmony, knowing that they love each other. Life is not like that, or if it is it happens by grace or accident, or perhaps because they are fond of you and you radiate warmth, loving acceptance and genuine interest in each of them, so that they are drawn home and tolerate each other for a while. There is a centrifugal force in families that pulls brothers, sisters, cousins, and their temporary and long-term partners away from each other. They often have different beliefs, life-styles and concerns. One may be passionately anti-abortion while another is committed to a woman's right to choose, one a born-again Christian and another a lesbian feminist. They have a right to their own beliefs, even if you profoundly disagree with them. Children and grandchildren are often forced to put on an act when they come home, and pretend that they like each other just to please granny. The result is a build-up of tension which leads to explosions. This is why family get-togethers are always tricky.

A wise grandmother learns never to cram the family together in a small space, and to plan ahead for a range of activities and a selection of choices when they come together: a walk in the countryside, Scrabble or stories round the fire, a science museum visit, a football match, theatre or concert, a barbecue in the garden, sledging in the snow or an outing to a wildlife park. Let them divide up and you enjoy them more. This applies even to meals. A buffet, in which people can mingle or move away from each other when they want to, may work better than a formal sit-down meal. You will need a table and appropriate seating for small children, but they enjoy selecting food, too. If your home is large enough, different things can be happening in different rooms: music in one, cooking and catching up with news in the kitchen, a group on the floor with a construction set or out on a climbing-frame or swing. Then you relax and enjoy them.

Grandmothers who at first feel relegated to the sidelines

often come to realize that they have been given a bandstand view of families in the process of change and can witness the amazing adaptability and creativity of human beings. 'I have learned the hardest part,' one woman concludes, 'letting go,' and this has given her fresh insight. Another says, 'I have learned to trust my daughters and to trust the life process.' Standing back, being, in one woman's words, 'more tuned in, light, relaxed and receptive', being 'laid-back and taking things as they come' gives space in which you can grow. Then what appears in the first shock of being a grandmother to be disempowerment becomes empowering.

Rediscovering yourself as a mother

A daughter having her first baby is often torn between a longing to be independent and to assert her own identity as an adult, on the one hand, and a need for dependency, on the other. This is an element in every girl's development from childhood to womanhood, whether or not she has children. It can lead to stresses in the relationship with her mother. You may think your daughter's behaviour is irrational and inconsiderate because one moment she seeks advice and the next moment rejects it, one day seems to want your help, and the next, criticizes you for offering it. This ambivalent relationship is one expression of the conflicts and confusion in growing from a child into a woman. She is in a state of transition – having to part with herself as a child. This is never easy, and the process may be very uncomfortable for all concerned. At times it is frightening for her to be alone, yet she is irritated by the feeling that she needs you. Part of her wants to be like you. Another part strives to resist being merged with you.

You will have worked through this transition yourself in your relationship with your mother as you grew up and had a child, and may remember how you felt. A woman who felt unloved as a child only discovered her mother as a friend when she had children, 'After a life-time of feeling neglected it was through my children's grandmother that I was able at last to find *my* mother. We were closest when enjoying them together. I could

appreciate her in her new role, and she responded with love.'
Her mother died and she comments, 'It is the grandparent in
my mother that I miss most of all . . . Some of the joy of being
a mother disappeared when my mother was no longer around
to enjoy them.'[12]

Each woman brings with her to grandmotherhood her past
experiences as both mother and daughter. This may mean
that if she had a difficult relationship with a mother who
was domineering or interfering she holds back, determined
not to intrude when her daughter seeks greater closeness. If
she felt deprived of emotional closeness with her mother she
hurries to offer help and advice when her daughter wants to
cope by herself.

You bring your own anxieties about mothering, too, the
doubts, fears and traumatic experiences through which you
lived as a mother. You carry with you, even after all these
years, the anxiety and pain which you felt when your children
were small, and it may unexpectedly erupt like a volcano that
you did not know was there, its rolling lava threatening your
relationship with your daughter. A woman whose first baby
had died with a heart condition at eight weeks, and was
told that she was starving her second baby, who had only
regained his birth weight at eight weeks, is understandably
anxious about her daughter's determination to breast-feed
and refusal to offer complementary bottle feeds. But knowing
that her daughter is getting good breast-feeding advice from a
counsellor, and seeing that the baby is bright-eyed and active,
she has learned not to express her anxieties and to support her
daughter in her commitment to breast-feeding.

Once you are aware of how past experience affects your
feelings and behaviour it becomes easier to do the right thing,
easier to negotiate with a daughter what she wants in any
particular situation, and to know the times when it is best to
offer help and when it is best to withdraw.

With your daughter's children you see your own mothering
in a new perspective. She may criticize you for what she thinks
was wrong in the way you brought her up, and draw contrasts
between your child-rearing practices and how *she* wants to be.
It can be a painful lesson. But as time passes and she mellows
as a mother, she is likely to become more tolerant and begin
to understand the dilemmas and challenges you faced, and

the constraints and stresses that affected your behaviour as a mother.

A grandmother often says that as she watches her daughter with her baby she finds her own mothering validated. A woman who always thought she had made a bad job of it comments, 'I'm feeling better about my own mothering.' Another remarks with surprise, 'I must have been a pretty good mum.'

But older women often still feel guilty about how they were as mothers, especially if they see their children managing to be more tolerant and relaxed with their children than they ever were, and finding ways of disciplining them without resorting to violence. A woman who is astonished at her daughter's capacity for warm, outgoing love, her sympathetic understanding of her children, and her complex mothering skills, says, 'I have learned to think of my daughter as almost more grown-up, certainly more responsible, than I have ever been.' One woman offers her daughter the ultimate accolade, 'I would have liked her to be *my* mother.' Annie's daughter is a single mother, and she and eighteen-month-old Billy live with her. 'It's a lovely relationship with the little one,' Annie says. 'As much as I loved my own children, I spent a lot of time nagging and scolding them. It was just me and the kids on my own. I was preoccupied with chores. I feel terribly guilty that I didn't make life a bit easier for them. I used to feel so tired and irritated. I'm tired (totally knackered sometimes!) but never irritated with Billy. I am much more tolerant. I have learned that I really am able to love.'

There is no recipe for success, there can be no instant solutions. But you can draw on your memories of being both mother and daughter to gain increased self-awareness and to better understand the experience a daughter is going through. In the process, emotional conflicts are resolved. This gives new zest to the challenging, exciting role of being a grandmother.

Nurturing yourself

When you have raised a family and experienced all the vicis-situdes, the alarms and the tragedy-comedy of mothering, you value yourself more. 'I have learned how to cope with anger when I can't meet their needs (or don't want to) . . . to let myself "off the hook",' one grandmother says. An important side-effect of the ability to stand back is that she is, for the first time in her life, making space for herself, and not always in the service of others. This does not mean that she is less ready to give time and devotion to and enjoy her grandchildren. What it does mean, however, is that she has not so totally invested in their lives that she neglects her own needs. She can observe more keenly, reflect with deeper understanding, and help more wisely, because she has her own space.

However you feel about being a grandmother, you can be sure that many other women share these emotions. If you veer between being pleased and irritated, confident and full of doubts, excited and depressed, at one time interested and another bored by the whole thing, know that this is normal, too. For most grandmothers, like mothers, do not step into their roles as instant stars. We *learn* to be grandmothers, just as we learned to be mothers.

Grandmother Skills

The professionalisation of care typical of Western and Northern cultures, means that both as mothers and grandmothers we are treated by experts as untrained amateurs. It is impossible to do away with *mothers* – we are needed for the sheer donkey-work of child-rearing, but grandmother care has become increasingly suspect. Most of us grandmothers do not have degrees in child psychology, nursing, nutrition, psychotherapy or teaching. We have not read the latest books on how to develop a child's potential and do not know the most recent systems of teaching reading, arithmetic or computer science. Unlike nursery school teachers, child therapists and paediatricians, we are amateurs.

In spite of Spock, Brazelton and Leach, a large proportion of the books on child-rearing seem to concentrate on how to produce a super-child who is academically gifted, amazingly creative and harmoniously socially adjusted. In bookshops and libraries and stacked on many mothers' book shelves are piles of instructional literature, ready to analyse harmful patterns of behaviour in the family, and reveal all the ways in which we women are supposed to damage our children, not only by what we do, but through our destructive patterns of thinking and feeling. These books systematically undermine our spontaneous ways of mothering and grandmothering. There is no way any of us can read them without being appalled at what our mothers and grandmothers did to us, severely critical of our own performance as mothers and grandmothers, and uncomfortably aware that we can never measure up, try as we might, to the standards of such professional advice. The result is not only that daughters often have little confidence in grandmother care, but that grandmothers themselves have lost confidence.

Many grandmothers also remember keenly the expert pronouncements on mothering that were imposed on them when they had young children. It is not only that they lack confidence now as grandmothers, but that their self-confidence as mothers was destroyed 30 or 40 years ago. They still bear the burden of theories based on the teachings of child-rearing specialists such as G. Stanley Hall, Truby-King and Mrs Frankenburg. So they are nervous about doing the wrong thing, offer 'treats' and are only marginally involved in their grandchildren's lives.

A TV show invited children to write in with letters and pictures describing what made their grandparents special. Many wrote about being given sweets and enjoying food, especially the younger ones. 'My Grandma makes me lots of scrumptious cakes. She lets me eat her cherries and currants. She lets me drink sherry'; 'My Grandma gives us strawberry jam every Saturday'; 'I like her apple crumble'; 'She makes lovely bilberry dumplings on special Sundays when it is someone's birthday or anniversary' and 'I love Nanny because she has lots of goodies in her fridge – not like our fridge'.

But much as they enjoy their food, some perceptive children made it clear that what they liked best was that grandparents gave their time and concentrated attention. Six year olds said, 'She's always got time for me' and 'My Nana and Grandad have time to spend with me and do special things with me', a seven year old said, 'She is always there when we need her.' Older children went into more detail: 'My grandma and grandad are special because they are always there when I need them and they always try to get to all my football matches even if it is cold and raining'; 'I love my Nan because even though she has lots of grandchildren she still has time for me. She plays lots of games with me and tells me stories of the old days. We sing lots of songs together.' A ten-year-old girl sums it up when she writes, 'The reason why I love my Grandmas so much is because they give us *Time*, especially the one who lives with me. *Time* to meet me from school and listen to my good and bad days. *Time* to teach me to make buns and cakes, sewing and knitting. *Time* to tell or read bedtime stories . . . Time is the best present to have.'[1]

Grandmothers can give far more than food, toys, the trip to Disneyland or a theme park, or an exciting holiday. We don't need to lay on a non-stop programme of entertainment when grandchildren visit. The most important things we can give are time and a genuine interest in what a child is doing.

In a disintegrated society children lack grandmothers, and

older women have no children to love. The city of Coventry faces many problems resulting from poverty and unemployment. Mothers are often little more than children themselves. Nerissa Jones, a priest in a deprived area of the city, runs a Granny Club for children which is proving highly successful. Older women – called The Grannies – come into the community centre to play with the children, give them a hug and listen to them. The children talk unreservedly to them and are also well-behaved because not only do the Grannies give them their undivided attention but they set sensible limits. Grannies and children draw, paint, do jigsaws, play house and model play dough together. It is simple and it works. Every child needs a grandmother.

The art of listening

When women talk about their own grandmothers the thing they value most was their readiness to listen and the obvious pleasure they took in listening. It is still true for grandchildren today. 'She listens to my jokes and laughs,' a six year old says, and a ten year old writes of her grandmother, 'She is very understanding, more than my Mum . . . I love my grandparents because they care about us and nothing is too much trouble for them, and they don't get angry.'

A busy mother often cannot make time to sit and listen, or is so preoccupied that she may not always hear what a child is saying. However busy you are when you are not with your grandchild, when you have the opportunity to be together you can use your listening skills. This is not always easy, if only because children do not expect adults to give them time and attention, and as they get older develop all sorts of ways of filling up boring encounters with them. They come into the house and turn on the TV straight away, or plonk themselves down to play computer games. After a long car journey to see you a younger child may be crotchety and vulnerable, or hyperactive and race round screaming. From about nine months, a baby who has not seen you for some time may be very suspicious of this strange woman, and definitely not want to be put in your arms, and an eighteen month old who does not visit you regularly may cling to a parent and cry when a mother tries to get to the bathroom. Mothers are sometimes apologetic about it, and feel that the grandmother is critical of the child who cannot let his mother out of his sight. You can make it clear that you do understand.

Building a relationship with a child does not happen instantly. Often children have other needs which must be dealt with first: to be changed, fed, have a nap, explore their immediate surroundings and feel safe in a different environment. They do not want to be stared at or swooped on and picked up or cuddled, or to have attention directed on to them while they explain what they did in school this week, or put on a star performance of a recitation or musical recital for grandma. If you do not see the children often, they need time to adjust. They may do this best while eating or playing in the bath or a pool.

An important element in active listening is respect for individual identity. When you had your own children it may have been quite difficult at first to believe in the inherent processes of growth and development. Many mothers, especially with their first child, are anxious to get on to the next stage, and concerned that it may not take place at the appropriate time. In the back of our minds there is often a picture of a 'normal' or 'ideal' child, a standard against which we measure our own, who is usually found wanting. We are busy with the hard work of child-rearing and all the worries and fears that this entails. Grandparents can be more detached. Experience and maturity give them perspective that enables them to enjoy their grandchildren for the individuals they are.

Though the grandmother stereotype is one of staid sobriety, you do not have to conform to it. You can encourage a sense of exploration and adventure. Christina Dodwell, the explorer, says of her grandmother that, 'She used to tell me, "If you don't try it, you'll never know if you like it." Her words came back to me when I was sharing bowls of maggots with the local people in New Guinea.'[2] You extend a child's horizons in the way that you comment on things that your grandchild says and in the questions you ask. You can stimulate imagination, prompt analytical thought, help a child become aware of the wider world, of social issues that are important, the needs of other people, and the implications of individual actions.

This is a vital element in moral and social development, and grandparents who give time to listen are uniquely placed to stimulate a child's questioning and creative thinking.

It may be impossible to have many face-to-face conversations with a grandchild because you live too far away, but there are other ways to keep in touch. If you like to draw, write illustrated letters and short stories, or you may find an audio-tape useful or a video. Record songs and rhymes in your own voice for a baby, stories and poems for a slightly older child, and letters full of news that really interests an older child. You may get a short tape in reply, but it should never become an onerous duty for a child, and the most you can expect is an occasional phone call.

Some grandparents are so isolated from their grandchildren that they would not know what to say on a tape. It helps to get to know children of the same age. They may be a neighbour's children, or a friend's grandchildren whom you baby-sit. Or you could volunteer to help with reading or with playground supervision in a school near you. Some church and community groups are glad to have grandmothers help with children's activities. This work is both rewarding in itself and enables you to understand and communicate better with your grandchildren. In fact, you may want to tape stories based on the personalities and adventures of the children with whom you are working, and each letter on tape from you becomes part of a long-running serial.

When a woman becomes a grandmother she may also have a great deal to give the new parents – and part of this is being there to listen to them, too, and to validate their experience.

Two of the most difficult things to learn are how to be silent and how to be relaxed. This is quite different from avoiding speaking while you are rigid with disapproval or anxiety, biting your lip to avoid blurting out what you *really* think, or scattering advice over everyone like a pepperpot. A relaxed silence means that you can hear and receive what people are saying in a way that is impossible if you are busily producing comment, suggestions, criticisms and what you think is helpful input of your own. A woman who had her mother to stay for three weeks described how every morning the first word she heard as she entered the kitchen and the last word when she went to bed at night came from her mother. Not words of wisdom or scintillating wit, but meaningless chatter, repetitive clichés and anecdotes about trivial episodes in her life that she had heard over and over again. It was driving her mad. The Victorians, who knew what it was to live in high-packed, overcrowded families, had an aphorism 'Silence is golden'.

You need to be aware of what your son and daughter want from you. This does not mean that you have to know everything that they are planning, or sit around waiting for disclosures and confessions, but that you are sensitive to how they are feeling and to the challenges they may be confronting – financial and career problems, for example, difficulties with the children, and concern about their education, development or behaviour. There is a world of difference between having empathy and snooping and prying. You may be aware of emotional undercurrents, perhaps in their own relationship, in which they do not want you to interfere, and because you can understand you know when to back off and keep quiet. It takes skill and self-control to listen in a reflective way, without rushing in with advice or comments. But if you are there for them when they want to talk, and you refrain from giving judgement or advice, you help them through at least some of the stressful experiences of parenthood. This is what non-directive counselling is all about.

The skills are not learned instantly and we all make mistakes when we attempt them, but they can strengthen your relationship with your children and grandchildren, and as you listen to them your understanding is deepened.

Any form of counselling tends to be seen nowadays as a technique reserved for professionals, for many functions which used to be normal parts of family life have been taken outside the family. Childbirth has been appropriated by obstetricians, healing by the medical system, education by schools and colleges, and counselling by psychologists and therapists.

A grandmother can offer a great deal simply by listening in a relaxed way. To listen with genuine interest is emotionally supportive, even when you have nothing else to give. Many times when I have listened to women who are confused or distressed I have felt utterly helpless to do anything to help. Afterwards they thanked me, and said that they had worked out what to do. Just being there for them, validating their own feelings and experiences, gave them confidence and helped them cope with a crisis or ordeal which previously overwhelmed them.

Motherhood is never an easy task, it is inherently stressful, and mothers of young children are often socially isolated and depressed. There is evidence that having young children is in itself so stressful that mothers with children under ten are more at risk of depression than at any other stage of a woman's life cycle. As a woman who has been through all this yourself, you have a lot to give your daughter or daughter-in-law. She may be experiencing very strong emotions and trying to cope with major problems in her life; she is anxious about a child, for example; she feels trapped by motherhood; she is depressed. You do not need to be a trained counsellor to listen wisely. The rules are simple:

- Never criticize.
- Never rush in with snap solutions, however obvious they may seem to be.
- Never attempt to psychoanalyse.
- Help to build up a woman's confidence in herself as a good mother, and reinforce her self-esteem.
- Accept your daughter or daughter-in-law as she is.
- Affirm *her* experience.

Sometimes questions are useful:

- What do you enjoy most about being a mother?
- Is there anything that you dislike about being a mother?
- Is there any way in which I could help with that?
- What would you like me to do more of?
- What would you like me to do less of?
- Is there anything that I have done already that you don't want me to do again?
- Is there anything that I don't do that you would appreciate me doing?
- Is there anything I do that you would like me to do in a different way?

Think back to the time when you had young children, how you felt about your mother and mother-in-law, what you wanted from each of them, and how they helped or failed to help. How would *you* have answered these questions?

Do not argue or protest about an answer a daughter or daughter-in-law gives. Accept them, then go away and think about them. They can help you get a fresh perspective on your role in the family. They may enable you to change in a positive way a relationship that has stuck in a rut or in which there are undercurrents of hostility.

When talking to anyone who is troubled, see if it helps to reflect back, as in a mirror, the stress, confusion, doubts and fears, or the pain that she is communicating. You need to do this without becoming overwhelmed by her suffering. Wait and let her take her own time to say whatever she wants to tell you. A discussion may take place face to face over a cup of tea or coffee, for example, or it may be easier when you are doing things together – in the kitchen, taking the children for a walk, sewing together, or in the car. You give encouragement by a nod, a questioning look or raising your eyebrows, and check that you understand what she is saying by asking now and again, 'Are you saying that . . . ?' and putting it into your own words. Sometimes you repeat her last phrase or word with an upward inflection, 'angry?', or 'feeling low?' There are occasions, too, when her irritated reaction helps to find a solution. You say something like, 'I get the feeling that you are worried about . . .', 'You seem tired . . .'. She snaps back, 'Of course I'm bloody well tired. I've been up six times in the night. How would *you* feel?' Then the time for listening is over. She needs *practical* help: take the baby for a couple of hours so that she can sleep or the older child for a day so that she can have uninterrupted time with the baby, pay for help in the house, get the laundry done without fuss, fill her freezer with meals that only need defrosting. When you are talking together you can also be quite straightforward, and if any subject might be too sensitive a one for her to discuss with you, ask, 'Do you want to talk about that, or not?' But the really important thing is not to let techniques dominate; instead show genuine empathy and be quick to see what she wants at the time.

The Story-teller

In societies all over the world story-tellers, older men and women who can tell the mixed myth and history of the tribe, of gods and goddesses, and the animals and plants on whom their peoples' lives depend, are highly respected. Through an oral tradition they pass on values that are important in the culture.

A grandmother may know how to hold an audience spellbound with tales of long ago, of how it was when she was a child, about her own grandmothers, about life as it was 40 or 50 years before her listeners were born. If she cannot tell stories at first hand, she can put them onto audio-tape or video. For story-telling is one of the undoubted skills of a successful grandmother. Acknowledging this, Club Med recruits grandmothers in its European resorts to tell stories to children and in return gives them free holidays.

Children themselves rate stories – especially the mixed myth and history of 'tales of olden days' – as a special ingredient of 'grandmother time'. These stories are often about their parents when they were young, sometimes about the grandmother herself when she was a girl, the naughty things she did, for example, and about boys and girls who did not have TV or video games, and the adventures they got up to. Under fives enjoy stories about themselves, real or fictitious. A photograph album can get you off to a good start, 'Once there was a little girl who . . .' and here is a picture of the little girl!

Not every grandmother knows how to tell stories. It is an art to be learned, and each of us has the raw material for them. With a child on your lap, cuddling up beside you in bed, or comfortable on a deep couch, you can recreate the past with all its excitement and drama, or you can let your imagination have free play and tell stories about animals, princes and princesses, robots or creatures from outer space.

The times for stories are when a child has been energetic and is ready for a quiet activity or whenever the mother needs a quiet space for herself. Never try to tear a child away from TV or video. Bide your time till the question comes, 'What can I do now?' or when a child is obviously at a loose end. A story makes a good finish to the day, and small children like cuddling into bed in the evening and entering a world of make-believe or other children's adventures. Bedtime stories should always be gentle and allow your listener to unwind from the tensions of the day.

A fifteen-minute story is long enough for under fives, whereas a five to eight year old can concentrate for half an hour or so. When you tell a story make sure the child is sitting comfortably first, give him or her your full attention, and encourage participation in the story-telling.

Decide exactly where to *begin*. A story needs a strong start to rivet a child's attention. Introduce each character clearly and vividly. Build up suspense till you get to the climax of the story, and then draw any loose strands together, resolve problems or dilemmas that the story has raised, and decide exactly where to stop. The skilful use of pause for emphasis, or to add suspense, together with lively facial expression, enriches the quality of your story-telling. Children love stories that are about familiar situations, objects, people and animals and that grow out of their own experience: food they like, favourite animals, an accident they had, and especially their own favourites.

If a grandchild is facing a particular challenge you may recall a similar incident from your own childhood around which you can weave a story: when you told a lie, got lost in a big store, had measles, went into hospital for an operation, or fell in the river. A grown-up granddaughter told me, 'We love the story of how, when my mum was a little girl, they all went out for a picnic and my mum fell in the stream and they had to go home. Gran had to tell it over and over again.' Explore ideas about stories that trace origins, too: how Great Grandpa and Great Grandma came to this country, how Granny and Grandpa met each other for the very first time, the story of how a nut grew into a big walnut tree, and fantastical stories, like echoes of Rudyard Kipling's *Just So* tales, about how the dog got her spots or how the baby owl learned not to be afraid of the dark. Stories about dreams – things that did not happen really – are ways of exploring powerful emotions that a child may be feeling: the boy who dreamed his baby brother turned into a pig, for example, or the child whose mummy disappeared in a puff of smoke. In dreams you can use magic to make everything all right in the end.

Small children love to have their stories repeated, and like phrases and sentences repeated within them. They also appreciate onomatopoeia – (when the sound imitates the sense), rhymes and other odd or funny sounds. If there are animals in a story an under five year old will love helping to make animal noises: sheep bleating, cows mooing, dogs barking, cats miaowing and snakes hissing. Starting at the child's level, gradually extend the vocabulary so that new words are learned. You can also ask questions which help the child to hook into a story, 'And what do you think was in that box?', 'Where did she hide?'

You may like to keep special books for when your grandchild visits, too. If you are unsure what to buy, your local children's librarian or bookseller will be a good source of advice on the range of books right for a child of that age and interests. Even babies enjoy books. You can start with board books that have bright, clear pictures of familiar objects. A baby whose attention has been captured may try to pick the pictures off the page, feel, rub or scrape them, or even eat them, but that does not matter. You can ask an eighteen month old, 'What is that?' and share the child's delight in naming an object. Your grandchild will probably want to turn the pages, exercising finger and thumb co-ordination. You can go on from naming objects to identifying colours, and at around two and a half years ask questions such as, 'Where does the dog live?', 'Whose house is that?' *'Then* what happens?' and 'So *what* did her mummy say?'

Two and three year olds also like picture books with some text and flaps to lift which reveal objects concealed underneath, and books with pictures which have different textures that can be touched. As a child learns to decipher words and begins to spell, rhymes are very useful, 'It's still dark, said the lark.' Four year olds enjoy counting the number of toys that the picture book child brings into bed, or the number of teddy bears that accumulate on each page. You can encourage a child's imagination by asking, 'And what do you think happened next?'

If you have a grandchild who is physically different from other children in any way you may be able to find books which address a child's feelings about being marked apart or second best, and which celebrate difference. There are also stories about fear of the dark, the first day at school, the birth of a sibling, moving house, being bullied at school, and the death of a pet or a loved person.

All over the world grandparents have been tellers of tales. Sitting in the chimney nook, by a camp fire, in a forest clearing or a desert tent, they have told fables about the origins of their people, the forces of good and evil, legends about animals, birds and fish, parables and sagas of their religion, and their relationship with the land or the sea. When you tell stories to your grandchild you join a glorious tradition of myth and make-believe.

Playing with babies

A bonus of becoming a grandmother and being with babies and toddlers is that you have an opportunity to rediscover the delights of play. 'It has taught me to give myself permission to break the rigid mould – to play before work is done.' A woman is able to relive her own early sensory experiences, exploring touch, taste, smell, sight and hearing as if for the very first time. It is not just that a grandmother enjoys entertaining her grand-child. She herself plays, and can do so unselfconsciously. All constraints of her life drop off as she crawls on the floor, barks or miaows, sings nonsense rhymes or blows raspberries on a baby's tummy. 'It's like seeing self when self was new-born – at three months, six months, one year and so on – a chance to capture my childhood again, and a perfect excuse to blow bubbles, play with clay, crayon and build forts.'

Time spent playing with a baby is precious: tickling games, peep-bo and pat-a-cake, water play at bath-time, meeting the baby in the mirror, copying each other's facial expressions, blowing bubbles, patting a ball, playing with balloons, bells and puppets, and all the games that entail taking turns 'Now me – now you' and a reciprocity which is the basis of human conversations.

Children have a vital need to play. Children's play is uni-versal. In tents in the desert, in sprawling shacks clinging to rubbish dumps in South America, in tenements in the inner city, in famine, war and appalling human disasters, in refugee camps, behind barred cots in orphanages in Romania, children play. When I was doing anthropological fieldwork in Jamaica I watched small children up in the hills whose only playthings were rocks, water, corn husks, a stone in an old tin can and a stick in the mud.

In play children learn to concentrate, persevere, overcome obstacles, consider options, solve problems. Play is work. They discover the qualities of tangible objects, how to understand size, weight, volume, balance – the basis of mathematics, engineering and architecture, and how to manipulate, by inter-locking, twisting, separating, deconstructing and recreating. They develop skills in motor co-ordination. They test out 'what if?' and learn to use their imagination. They build their own worlds, shaping reality in the ways *they* want and so grow in self-confidence and the capacity for independent action and autonomy. In re-enacting experiences in play, they come to terms with them, including traumatic experiences. They test out possibilities. They develop the skills that adults have, as they imitate our actions. When they play with other children they learn to negotiate and to share – the basis of all other social skills.

It is important that we respect children's play, observe and learn from it, and never interrupt play without good reason.

Even before a baby is three months old, the age at which she often begins to grasp an object, you can begin to play together by exploring different textures: soft, hard, squashy, slippery, rough and smooth; a piece of velvet, a soft woollen shawl, silver foil, sandpaper; objects that move and those that are fixed, things that are warm and cold, things that make a noise (a tin containing buttons or pebbles, firmly sealed with sticky tape, for instance) and others that make no sound. You can smell mint, lemon, coffee, pineapple, sweet basil, garlic or a rose. You sniff it yourself and then see her screw up her nose as well. You are aware that the freshness and clarity of your own senses is opening up to new experiences of sight, touch, hearing, smell and taste.

It is not only babies who learn through play. *You* learn, too. You learn how to engage with the baby, to give and take, observe each phase of development and find out what the child likes and is able to achieve at this stage; you explore new ways of enjoying each other, and discover that child's unique personality.

With a baby on your knee, or sitting face to face, there are dozens of action rhymes you can play together. There are hand-clapping games like pat-a-cake and actions to accompany the hymn 'If you're happy and you know it, clap your hands', bouncing games such as:

> *Handy-Spandy, jack-a-dandy*
> *loved plum cake and sugar candy.*
> *He bought some at a grocer's shop,*
> *and then he goes*
> *hop, hop-a-hop'* with a final lift up in the air.

There are toe-wiggling games such as, 'This little piggy went to market', foot-patting games like:

> *Diddle-diddle dumpling*
> *My son John*
> *Went to bed with his trousers on,*
> *One shoe off and one shoe on,*
> *Diddle-diddle dumpling*
> *My son John.*

The baby can ride on your knee, gently at first, then more vigorously as you say, 'A farmer went riding', finally holding the child under her arms as you drop her between your knees all of a sudden. Then there is, 'This is the way the ladies ride . . .' and 'To market, to market, to buy a fat pig . . .' There are tickling games like 'Round and round the garden goes the teddy bear' and games with hand and arm movements:

> *Incy wincy spider, climbing up the spout.*
> *Down came the rain and washed pour Incy out.*
> *Out came the sun and dried up all the rain.*
> *And Incy wincy spider climbed up the spout again.*

And rocking games:

Row, row, row your boat,
Gently down the stream,
Merrily, merrily, merrily, merrily,
Life is but a dream.

Playing with a baby is not playing to win, or demonstrate expertise, or improve skills, but playing for the sheer fun of it. There are no rules to learn – or perhaps it is more accurate to say that the rules that determine how we play with babies lie hidden in our culture. It is part of an oral tradition of mothering and grandmothering, which is shared with aunts and other women in the family too. Many games were known, even if in a slightly different form, by our own grandmothers and great-grandmothers, and often theirs before them.

When you play with babies you dip into this rich tradition and join a dance of interaction that women have passed down since mothers and grandmothers first devised the games that have lasted, almost unchanged, for hundreds of years.

Water play

Water has the power to relax, fascinate and excite a child. If you have a garden, a hose with a sprinkler and a paddling pool provide fun on a hot day. Your bathroom can also be turned into a water play centre. Never leave a child unattended with water, not only for his own safety, but also for the sake of your possessions.

In the kitchen you can find things to turn into water toys: a plastic jug, corks, a ladle, funnels, a sieve and colander, some plastic bottles and containers of different sizes, a bottle that will squirt in a satisfying way, a sponge, things that float and things that sink. Bath and pool toys that you can buy include ducks, sailing boats and powered boats, ping-pong balls, plastic watering cans, water pistols, and water mills, wheels and chutes.

Bubble mixture can be made with one part washing up detergent to two parts water. Garden wire can be bent to form a blower (or a sparkling wine bottle top with the cap removed). Blowing through straws into soapy water is fun too.

When a grandchild is being difficult or seems bored or unhappy, see what happens when you put her in the bath or pool. Energetic splashing releases tension and soothes a temper tantrum better than anything else. The improvement is often instantaneous.

Make-believe

Children like to have their own small world into which they can crawl: a Wendy house, tent, tree house, outdoor shed, or climbing-frame with an enclosed area or a tarpaulin thrown over. They enjoy building boundaries and having space which belongs to them alone. It could be a simple construction of chairs or other furniture, a grand piano for instance with blankets or sheets thrown over it. Or they could build a cardboard house from large boxes, with openings leading from one to another. If you have no large boxes handy, any shop that sells major electrical equipment – fridges, cookers, washing machines and dishwashers – will provide them, and may invite you to go through their skip. With a sleeping bag or blanket, a child can have a bed inside. A torch, dolls and furry animals add to the fun.

Chairs and tables can also be used to construct a boat, plane or train, with dolls or soft toys as passengers. Out of doors, logs of different sizes, wooden tubs, planks and boxes can be used to make houses or a jungle adventure course linked by stepping stones or bricks embedded firmly in earth, and with ropes hanging from branches.

Imaginative play is stimulated by having a dressing-up box, with hats, masks, old clothes, table-cloths and curtains, strips of fabric, artificial flowers, feathers, scarves, shoes, handbags, spectacle frames and ribbons. Inside a small box store broken 'jewellery' and some Christmas tree ornaments that are not fragile, and have large safety pins ready for fixing robes and capes. Crowns can be cut from thin card and decorated with gold paint, glued-on glitter or felt tip.

A puppet theatre can be constructed from a large box or small crate too. But this is not an occupation for a solitary child – puppets need an audience. Glove puppets or puppets on solid sticks can be stuffed with kapok or old tights. If you keep a scrap basket of fabric, bits of wool, felt for animal ears, and buttons for eyes and mouths, cotton wool for beards, wool or string for hair, and tights that can be cut up and plaited to make pigtails, you can invent together a wide range of characters.

Once a child is past the stage of putting everything in her mouth a sand-tray or pit is good for imaginative play too. Even an old tyre filled with sand will do. From the age of two or three a child will construct her own small world through twigs, leaves, pebbles, plastic yoghurt cups, model animals and miniature houses and people, and a supply of water is useful for making rivers and ponds.

Kitchen magic

Any kitchen is a treasure house of containers of different shapes and sizes, saucepans to bang with a spoon, jars to fill with peas, cans to stack, beans and lentils to rattle and pour, jars to learn to unscrew, a dustpan and brush to sweep and – beware – drawers and cupboards to open and shut, and to empty of their contents, and machinery which only needs the press of a button to whirr into action. Make it clear from that the start that some cupboards are out of bounds and ensure that children do not play with, spill or drink dangerous cleaning substances and sprays. Bear in mind all the time that safety is a prime consideration.

Consider keeping a special cupboard of playthings. If you have more than one grandchild you may be able to make space for play materials suitable for different ages. Store with these the old shirts and waterproof aprons that they will need if they want to work in the kitchen. Waterproof cuffs to wear over the ends of their sleeves are also a good idea.

You need not be an expert chef to teach a child to enjoy cooking, but you do need to tolerate dough, flour and dried fruit turning up in unexpected places for days after. There is a long tradition of grandmothers letting children help with baking, and when adults recall their grandmothers this is for many an abiding memory. Granny food is 'soul food', the stuff of tradition. Start with simple tasks such as making a sandwich and spreading softened butter, soft cheese or peanut butter. If you are making a fruit salad the child can peel the banana and slice fruit. As he becomes more expert with a knife other things can be sliced too, including hard cheeses and vegetables. Then there are other activities such as grating cheese, carrot or apples, dipping in olive oil, chopping vegetables, mashing potatoes and other root vegetables, sprinkling chopped nuts, seeds and Parmesan, making toast, using a rolling pin, and electrical equipment such as the grill, the oven, the microwave, and the dishwasher, and knowing which buttons to press and which knobs to turn. Whisking and beating butter, eggs or cream needs the right wrist movement. My granddaughter Laura learned this before she was a year old by watching and imitating me, and enjoyed having a large, shiny copper bowl and an old-fashioned hand whisk which made a pleasant ringing noise as she used it to beat busily. A child goes from there to whisking up soap bubbles, and then to eggs and pancake batter.

Bread dough can be kneaded vigorously and rolled between a child's hands into long snakes, shaped into knots, cottage loaves, twists and plaits, and with grandmother's help turned into stars, hedgehogs, tortoises, a family of bears, men and women, or the letters of the alphabet. Read a story, do some gardening together or go out for a walk while the dough is rising to double its size. The proved dough can then be painted with beaten egg and sprinkled with poppy, sesame or sunflower seeds. You can add butter, sultanas, beaten eggs and chopped nuts to the dough, or roll out a long rectangle and invent savoury fillings that a child can spread over with a spatula before rolling the dough up like a swiss roll.

Children who don't much enjoy vegetables may accept them in this form: spinach purée with nutmeg and chopped fried onions, sun-dried tomatoes soaked in olive oil with minced garlic and basil, cheese and onion, crushed walnuts in olive paste, sautéed chopped mushrooms, to which pine kernels and herbs such as marjoram, rosemary and sage can all be added. And the smells are wonderful. Cleaning up the kitchen should be made part of the fun, and if you are going to eat what you have cooked together, laying the table is an additional learning experience.

Biscuit making, either sweet or savoury, gives an opportunity to use pastry cutters of different sizes and shapes to make smiling faces or a house with currants and cherries, angelica and chopped nuts, or with grated cheese, herbs, slivers of sun-dried tomato and celery seeds and nuts.

With pastry a child can make tarts which, after being baked blind, can be filled with spiced apple purée, an onion and cheese custard mixture, or jam. Leftover bits will make basic cheese straws, though by this time, shaped by hot little hands, they may be rather heavy. Then there are more complicated things like gingersnaps, to be curled round wooden spoon handles, or a gingerbread house, iced and decorated with hundreds and thousands, coloured sweets and chocolate drops.

From about five years old your grandchild can learn how to use an electric mixer safely. Sam, my grandson, invented his Nutty Nibbles at this age. Here is his recipe dictated in his own words:

Sam's Nutty Nibbles

> *Bread – brown and crusty – 2 cups*
> *Nuts – 1 cup*
> *Cheese – 1 cup*
> *Butter – 1 teaspoon*
> *Salt and pepper – to taste*
> *Herbs – to taste: celery seeds, lemon, basil and dill*
> *1 macaroon*

Preheat the oven to 200°C.

> *Break up the bread and put it in a Magimix. Turn on the Magimix. When the bread has turned into small crumbs turn off the Magimix. Put all the other ingredients in the bowl and turn on the Magimix. When the mixture looks like fine crumbs again turn off the Magimix.*

> *Take a spoonful of the mixture and squeeze it between your hands in the shape of a fat biscuit. Place these biscuits onto a baking tray and put them into the hot oven.*

> *After 10 minutes, when the biscuits are brown at the*

edges, take them out of the oven. Allow the Nutty Nibbles to cool for 5 minutes before eating them.

If you have a pasta machine you can devise different coloured pastas, mixing them with carrots, beetroot or spinach, and produce a variety of shapes, draping them over wire or wooden coat hangers to dry.

Children enjoy stuffing anything, and can invent weird and wonderful mixtures, bound with cream cheese, sour cream, butter or concentrated tomato purée, for filling baked potatoes, putting inside rings of mashed carrots, swede, parsnips, or whatever other vegetables they like.

If a child has a restricted diet because he distrusts any food that is not pasta, pizza or potatoes, for instance, cooking together is an opportunity to explore new tastes and mixtures in a situation in which *he* is in control. 'Do you think you need more lemon juice in there? See if it tastes better with a little tahini . . . We could try roasted pine kernels on top.'

Talk about where foods come from, the people who produce the basic foodstuffs, those who especially like any particular food – tortillas, frogs' legs and snails, curry, octopus and polenta, for example – and introduce a child to the basic chemistry of cooking: the qualities of eggs, yeast, baking powder, the effects of heating and freezing, and – if you can do it without preaching – the vitamins and minerals in fruit and vegetables. Do not force information. Pick up on a child's interests, rather than give a lesson.

As children get older they learn a lot. By the time a child is five or six this involves learning the skills of careful planning ahead, being organized, reading, writing and arithmetic. Some children like to construct imaginary menus. Sam drew a picture of a teddy bear's picnic with all the food laid-out on a cloth in the middle and carefully labelled each dish. Weighing and measuring, grouping things that are the same size, cutting with sharp knives, pouring carefully, putting things away after use, clearing up spills immediately, observing rules of safety when handling knives and hot pans, reading a recipe, putting an invented recipe on the word processor, are all part of learning to work in the kitchen. Children can compile their own illustrated recipe book. The back of printout paper or off-cuts from a printer's can be punched and string or wool threaded through to make the book.

Growing things

Grandmothers are often the ones who introduce the pleasures of gardening to their grandchildren. You do not even need a garden. A window-box kept especially for plants that give quick results will do, or some pots on the kitchen window-sill. You can grow things to eat: peppery nasturtium flowers, marigold petals, and chives to sprinkle on salads.

When they are around five children can have a strawberry pot on a patio or veranda, and in the winter a forced hyacinth in a glass jar so that they can see the roots develop. With careful timing it will flower at Christmas. They might plant bowls of daffodils, narcissi, or bright red tulips that will bloom in late winter. This way you can show the children how to look after growing things.

Cress can be grown on damp blotting paper, a wad of kitchen paper or a synthetic sponge. First soak the surface, then press out the excess water and sprinkle the seeds over it. They could be in the shape of a face or the letters or initials of the child's name. The seeds will start to sprout within a week if kept warm and damp. Cress can also be grown on pottery hedgehogs and pigs sold in garden centres, or in empty eggshells stuffed with damp cotton wool. The child can paint a funny face with felt-tips on the egg first and the eggshell person will grow green hair.

The best way to grow peas or broad beans so that the child can see the plants develop is in a jam jar lined with damp kitchen paper. First soak the peas or beans in water for twenty-four hours, then pour about two fingers' width of water into the bottom of the jar and place the beans and peas between the paper and the glass, leaving space for the roots to grow down and the shoots to uncurl upwards; finally put the jar by a window so that the child can see what is happening.

Making things

For a grandmother who is an artist or craftswoman herself it can be agonizing to watch a child struggle with the first stages of knowing how to use paints or clay, and frustrating when it proves impossible to work alongside a little person who is making a great deal of mess and keeps on invading your territory and wanting your attention and help. So keep child-centered creativity to its own time and do not attempt to do your own work simultaneously.

The cardinal rule is to get all the material that will be needed ready first. If you go off to find tools, for instance, by the time you get back or turn round from hunting in a cupboard, there may be chaos or the child may have wandered off bored. Make each activity step by step, and clear up together as you go along. Do not expect a child to concentrate for longer than about ten minutes. If it is a messy job, protect furniture, floor and walls with sheets of plastic, newspaper and cardboard, and have a bowl of soapy water and a flannel to hand. In summer you can organize creative activity out of doors, where any mess is much easier to clean up. A two year old with a painting easel in the garden has far more freedom than in the kitchen. Make collections of raw materials for activities and keep them in a special box or cupboard: paints, brushes, old tights, gloves and socks, scraps of fabric and boxes, for example. Adapt the project to the age of the child. For instance, a three year old can use felt-tips to make paperbag masks. For a cat or dog twist the corners for ears and fix them with rubber bands. A four year old can sew a red woolly mouth and button eyes on an old sock to make a hand puppet, and could try sticking or sewing a red tongue in the middle of the mouth. Show the child how to put his hands round and draw the mouth in between forefinger and thumb to make the animal 'talk'. A five year old can use scissors to cut a cardboard mask out of a paper plate or box, with a hole in each ear through which you thread elastic to hold it in place, or slot large rubber bands to attach it to her ears. She can paint on a face, the nose could be a cardboard flap, a bottle top or cork, the hair string, raffia, wool or paper strips twisted round a pencil to make them curly, while felt, straws for whiskers and cotton wool for fur can make animal masks.

Big sheets of lining paper or old wallpaper are useful. The child lies down on a sheet on the floor, stretching out her arms and legs, while you use a felt-tip to draw her outline. Then she completes the picture with a face, hair, clothes and so on.

Make simple cut-out stencils of birds, animals, flowers, the sun, the moon and the stars. A child can produce repeated patterns on paper or, if you have fabric paints, on cotton, on birthday cards and party invitations. Help the child find leaves that are heavily veined to make leaf prints. Cut geometric and heart shapes in a cross-section of potato, blot dry, and make potato prints.

You can make collage pictures too. Cut out in cardboard the shape of a tree, fish, bird, house, animal or person. The child sticks on fabric pieces, shapes from a packet of gummed, coloured paper, or cut shapes from a glossy magazine, to decorate it. Some glitter can be fun too. For a bird the child may be able to find a few feathers out of doors. If you make a hedgehog shape, drinking straws can be cut and stuck on as prickles. Sheep can be covered with cotton wool tufts.

One of the simplest ways of using strips of paper is to make paper people. Cut a long chain of paper children holding hands by folding a rectangle of newspaper or lining paper into a concertina shape; then draw a child on the end piece and cut round it. Unfold and the child can draw faces on the people and colour them.

With a scrap-book and photographs a child could construct a story of a special holiday, how she grew from a baby to an eight year old, or a story about the family and some of their adventures and experiences.

Miniature gardens can be made in baking tins or aluminium foil dishes. The child needs to collect moss, small stones and twigs, and pick violets, primroses, buttercups and other small flowers. Several toy animals from a farmyard set or Noah's Ark can be placed in the garden.

With a store of modelling clay or play dough you have creative material ready in the kitchen for times when you want to concentrate on cooking without an eager helper. You can put together home-made play dough with half a kilo of flour, about half as much salt to flour, two dessertspoons of cream of tartar, and water to mix (about a large cupful). If you add a little oil the mixture will be easier to work. Knead it together, then plop it in a big saucepan and heat it gently, stirring, until it cooks into a ball of dough that comes away from the sides of the pan. Tip it out and let it cool until you can handle it, then knead it to a smooth dough. This will keep for about twelve weeks in a sealed polythene bag or plastic box in the fridge.

Young children like to squash, pinch, squeeze, bang and roll play dough. Older children can make bowls, dolls, house furniture, people, food and animals, a miniature village, planes, spacerockets, trains and cars, and angels for the Christmas tree. Models can be baked in a hot oven until they are hard, and then painted with poster paints or acrylics. For older children you can also buy modelling clay that is cooked in an ordinary oven.

This may all sound trivial. Listening to children, telling stories, playing games, singing rhymes, making messes in the kitchen, fiddling around with clay – anyone can do that. Perhaps. But many people do not – even those who have jobs caring for children. It is possible to be with children and fail to engage with them, not communicate with them, not be emotionally in touch, not to validate them as people.

I sat in a playground in New York's Central Park. It was for an interview with a *New York Times* journalist who thought that the photograph of me to accompany her piece would be best if children were included in the scene. You don't see children in the streets of New York. The only place to go is somewhere where kids are corralled. Hence the playground. There were few mothers with their children, only one granny, and the other dozen or so children were being supervised by 'nannies'. To me, coming from England, they did not seem to look or behave like nannies. There are many warm and wonderful nannies, but these were bored, detached, the muscles of their faces slack and expressionless. Perhaps they were depressed. They were certainly out of touch with their charges. Child care was obviously a tedious chore that somehow had to be endured. They did not talk to the children, they just gave orders. They did not cuddle them, they often did not even look at them. When the children cried, they did not comfort them. When a child did something that made him happy – reached the top of the climbing-frame, for instance – they did not join in his happiness, or even acknowledge it.

A two year old was distressed and had been crying non-stop for half an hour. I learned later that he was one of twins and had never been separated from his twin before. He had been brought to the play area and plonked in a swing, and he screamed till I thought he was going to vomit. The woman in charge of him stood at the side of the swing, pushing it back and forwards, ignoring him while she continued a desultory conversation with friends.

Meanwhile the granny was running round bright-eyed and sharing in the excitement of her grandchild's discoveries and achievements. Here was one-to-one child-centred care given by a woman who was enjoying it, entering the fun with a grandchild who was exploring and learning with loving encouragement. It provided dramatic contrast between two kinds of child care.

Grandmother care is under-valued and often despised. There must be some grandmothers who haven't a clue about how to care for grandchildren. There are certainly grandmothers who do not want to, or whose lives are so busy that they cannot possibly fit in grandchild care as well. But many grandmothers love it and are eager to make time to be with their grandchildren. There are many warm and wonderful nannies. Yet observing babies and small children with nannies and *au pairs*, with minders and day-care providers in many countries – Russia, Eastern and Western Europe, the Mediterranean countries, Israel, the Caribbean and the USA – I have come to the conclusion that grandmother care is often among the best kinds of child care, even if that is only possible for a few hours at a time and mothers at work must rely on other people to be the primary care providers.

To become a grandmother gives us the chance to rediscover ourselves as mothers, to be reborn as mothers. Becoming a grandmother makes it possible to rediscover our own childhood, to be reborn as a child.

Whether you are crouching with a small child inside a house made by draping a sheet over a table or a group of chairs, or concentrating on all the tiny details of a ladybird that has perched on your hand or a trail of ants winding through the earth and round blades of grass, or singing raucous, silly songs and making up the rhymes as you go along, or discussing very seriously goodies and baddies on a children's TV programme, you are privileged to share a child's world and be part of that world yourself. It is a second chance to find again a child's sense of wonder, and to see that world as if for the very first time. Blake's lines are often quoted, so have lost some of their jewel-bright intensity – yet:

> To see a World in a grain of sand,
> And a Heaven in a wild flower,
> Hold Infinity in the palm of your hand,
> And Eternity in an hour . . .[3]

This is the opportunity you have as a grandmother.

References

Chapter 1

1 Leni O'Connell, 'A second parenthood', *Independent on Sunday*, 6 February 1994
2 Helena Lopata, *Occupation: Housewife*, OUP, Oxford, 1971
3 Janet Mansfield, *Good Housekeeping*, February 1993, pp. 97
4 Alma H Bond, *On becoming a Grandparent: a diary of family discovery* Bridge Works Publishing, New York, 1994, pp. 7–8

Chapter 2

1 Louis M Hellman and Jack Pritchard (eds), *Williams Obstetrics*, 4th edn, Appleton-Century-Crofts, New York, 1971, p. 1096
2 Coney Sandra, *The Menopause Industry: A guide to medicine's 'discovery' of the mid-life woman*, The Women's Press, London, 1995
3 Sheila Kitzinger, *Woman's Experience of Sex*, Penguin, London, 1985
4 Terry McCarthy, 'Noisy welcome from the bath house woman', *Independent*, 16 December 1991
5 Jasper Rees, 'The great white gets a seal of approval', *Independent*, 15 April 1995
6 Profile, *Options*, September 1995
7 Alma H Bond, *op.cit.*, p. 55
8 Catherine MacKinnon, '1982 Feminism, Marxism, Method and State: Agenda for theory', *Signs*, 7, 3, pp. 534–5
9 Bond, *op.cit.*, p. 712

Chapter 3

1 Bernice Andrews, *British Psychology Society Conference*, London, December 1994

2 *I Love my Granny and Grandpa too*, TV-am and Robson Books, London, 1989

3 Lillian E Troll, 'Grandparenting' in L W Poon (ed), *Aging in the 1980s: psychological issues*, APA, Washington DC, 1980

4 L Harris & Associates, *The Myth and reality of ageing in America*, National Council on Ageing, New York, 1975

5 Annette Kienz, *Guide des grands-mères*, Herme, Paris, 1988

6 'Child Health and Protection', supplement to *US Daily*, 5, 28 November 1930, p. 18

7 William H Chafe, *The American Woman: Her changing social, economic and political roles 1920–1970*, OUP, New York, 1972, p. 164

8 Geraldine Youcha, *Minding the Children*, Scribner, New York, 1995, p. 327

9 Interview with Laura Cao Romero

10 *Social trends 1995*, Central Statistical Office, London, 1995

11 Celia Dodd, 'When did you last see your grandchildren?', *Independent*, 22 September 1993

12 Julie Myerson, *Independent*, 22 January 1996

13 Celia Dodd, *op.cit.*

14 *Social trends 1995 op. cit.*

15 Brenda Houghton, 'Developing Step by Step', *Independent on Sunday Magazine*, 6 February 1994

16 *I Love my Granny and Grandpa too, op. cit.*

17 Laura Kelly, *Bad Chemistry*, HarperCollins, London, 1994, p. 186

18 Leni O'Connell, 'A second parenthood', *Independent on Sunday*, 6 February 1994

19 Pollock and J Vaughan (eds), *A Lesbian Parenting Anthology*, Firebrand, New York, 1987, pp. 202–6

20 Faith Reboin, 'Lesbian/Grandmother' in Pollock and J Vaughan (eds), *A Lesbian Parenting Anthology*, Firebrand, New York, 1987, pp. 202–6

21 Miranda France, 'The Missing Children of Argentina', *Marie Claire*, May 1992; France, 'Children who choose to live with their parents' persecutors', *Marie Claire*, March 1995

22 Nelida de Navajas in interview, quoted in Rita Arditti and M Lykes, M Brinton, 'Recovering identity: the work of the Grandmothers of Plaza de Mayo', *Women's Studies International Forum*, vol 5, 4, 1992, pp. 461–71

23 Arditti and Lykes, *ibid.*

24 Peter Simple, 'Way of The World', *Sunday Telegraph*, 12 February 1995

24 Julia Neuberger, 'A Childhood', *Times Magazine*, 11 February 1995

25 *Inquiry into the Third Age*, Report No 9, Carnegie Trust, Nuffield Department of Clinical Medicine, Oxford, 1992

26 *Report of the Advisory Group on Osteoporosis*, Department of Health, London, 1995

27 John L C Dall, 'The Greying of Europe', *British Medical Journal*, 309, 1994, pp. 1282–5

Chapter 4

1 Julie Burchill, 'Never too old? You are sometimes', *Independent*, 10 September 1995

2 Margaret Atwood, *Bodily Harm*, Random House, New York, 1983
3 Christina Gombar, 'The end of the reign of Queen Helen' in Valerie Kack-Brice (ed), *For She is the Tree of Life: grandmothers through the eyes of women writers*, Conari Press, Berkeley, 1994, pp. 154–7
4 Gloria Hunniford quoted by Richard Barber, 'Our mother would laugh at this', *Chic*, October 1995
5 John Tovey, *A Feast of Vegetables*, Century, London, 1985, p. 203
6 M F K Fisher, 'Grandmother's nervous stomach', *To Begin Again*, University of Pittsburgh Press, Pittsburgh, 1993
7 Shashi Deshpande, 'Of kitchens and goddesses' in Antonia Till (ed), *Loaves and Wishes*, Virago, London, pp. 17–18
8 Jackie E Fox, 'In memory of Rose' in Susan L Aglietti (ed), *Filtered Images: women remembering their grandmothers*, Vintage '45 Press, Orinda, California, 1992, p. 172
9 Joanne Seltzer, 'Grandma, I too am a grandma' in Aglietti (ed), *op. cit.*, p. 182

Chapter 5

1 Mernissi Fatima, *The Harem Within*, Doubleday, London, 1994
2 S Chirawatkul and L Manderson, 'Perceptions of menopause in Northeast Thailand: Contested meaning and practice', *Social Science & Medicine*, Vol 39, 11, 1994, pp. 1545–54
3 John F Embree, *A Japanese Village*, Kegan Paul, London, 1946
4 Isaac Schapera, *Married Life in an African Tribe*, Pelican, London, 1971
5 Beverley Chalmers, *African Birth: Childbirth in cultural transition*, Berev Publications, PO Box 107, River Club South Africa, 1990, pp. 22–3
6 Chalmers, *ibid.*, pp. 54–5
7 Dorothea Sich, 'Conflict between modern obstetrics and East Asian traditional birthing systems: the Korean case' in Ogawa, Teizo (ed), *History of Obstetrics: Proceedings of 7th International Symposium on Comparative History of Medicine – East and West*, Taniguchi Foundation, Osaka, 1982
8 Sarah E Castle, 'Child fostering and children's nutritional outcomes in rural Mali: the role of female status in directing child transfers', *Social Science & Medicine*, Vol 40, 5, March 1995, pp. 679–93
9 V W Turner, *The Drums of Affliction: A study of religious processes among the Ndembu of Zambia*, OUP, Oxford, 1968
10 Gary Witherspoon, 'A New Look at Navajo Social Organisation', *American Anthropologist*, 70, 1970
11 Louise Lamphere, 'Women in domestic groups' in Rosaldo Michelle Zimbalist and Louise Lamphere (eds), *Woman, Culture and Society*, Stamford University Press, Palo Alto, 1974
12 James Siegel, *The Rope of God*, Berkeley, California, 1969
13 Raymond T Smith, *The Negro Family in British Guiana: Family structure and social status in the villages*, Routledge, London, 1956
14 Smith, *ibid.*

15 Margery Wolf, *Women and the Family in Rural Taiwan*, Stamford University Press, 1972
16 Wolf, *ibid.*
17 Anne Baring and Jules Cashford, *The Myth of the Goddess: Evolution of an Image*, Viking, New York, 1991
18 Quoted by Geoffrey Parrinder, *Witchcraft: European and African*, Penguin, London, 1958

Chapter 6

1 P Schroeder, 'Infertility and the world outside', *Fertility & Sterility*, vol 49, 765, 1988
2 Alma H Bond, *op.cit.*, p. 2
3 Bond, *op.cit.*, p. 28
4 Bond, *op.cit.*, p. 2
5 Linda M Whitford and Lori Gonzalez, 'Stigma: The hidden burden of infertility', *Social Science & Medicine*, vol 40, 1, 1995, pp. 27–36
6 *Hello*, 2 July 1994
7 Lisa Hilboldt, 'Baby Beauty Contest', *Marie Claire*, October 1994

Chapter 7

1 J de Boulay, *Portrait of a Greek Mountain Village*, OUP, Oxford, 1974
2 Muriel Spark, *The Prime of Miss Jean Brodie*, Penguin, London, 1965, p. 11
3 Lesley Doyal, *What Makes Women Sick: Gender and the political economy of health*, Macmillan, London, 1995, p. 28
4 Elyse Ann Barnett, 'Notes on nervios: A disorder of menopause', *Health Care For Women International*, 10, Nos 2 & 3, 1989, pp. 159–69
5 P Cotterill, '"But for Freedom, You see, Not to be a Babyminder": Women's attitudes towards a grandmother care', *Sociology*, 26, 4
6 'Unplanned parenthood', *Sunday Times Style*, 26 February 1995

Chapter 8

1 Interview with Laura Cao Romero
2 Ellen Judith Reich, *Waiting: a diary of loss and hope in pregnancy*, Haworth Press, New York, 1992, p. 44
3 Nicky Leap and Billie Hunter, *The Midwife's Tale*, Scarlett Press, London, 1993, p. 20

4 Leap and Hunter, *op.cit.*, p. 33
5 Marie O'Connor, *Birth Tides*, Pandora, London, 1995
6 O'Connor, *ibid.*
7 Sheila Kitzinger, *Being Born*, Dorling Kindersley, London, 1990
8 Hope Edelman, *Motherless Daughters: The Legacy of Loss*, Addison Wesley, New York, 1994
9 Edelman, *op.cit.*, p. 243

Chapter 9

1 G Hagestad, 'Patterns of communication and influence between grandparents and grandchildren in a changing society', paper presented at World Congress of Sociology, Sweden, 1978

Chapter 10

1 Rubin J Provenzanof Luriaz, 'The eye of the beholder: parents' views on sex of newborns', *American Journal of Ortho-Psychiatry*, 44, 4, pp. 512–19, 1974
2 Leiderman P Thomane & J Olson, 'Neonate-mother interaction during breast feeding', *Developmental Psychology*, 6, pp. 110–18, 1972
3 J A Will, P A Self and N Datan, 'Maternal behavior and perceived sex of infant', *American Journal of Ortho-Psychiatry*, 46, 1, pp. 135–9, 1976
4 O R Fischer, 'Mothers and Mothers-in-law', *Journal of Marriage and the Family*, 45, pp. 187–92, 1983; J F Robertson, 'Grandmotherhood: A study of role conceptions', *Journal of Marriage and the Family*, 39, pp. 165–74, 1977; Kahana and Kahana E, 'Theoretical and research perspectives on grandparenthood', *Aging and Human Development*, 2, 4, pp. 261–8, 1971; S Cunningham-Burley, 'Constructing Grandparenthood: Anticipating appropriate action', *Sociology*, 19.3, pp. 421–36, 1985
5 C Delphy and D Leonard, *Familiar Exploitation: A new analysis of marriage and contemporary western societies*, London, Polity Press, 1992
6 L Troll and B Turner, 'The effect of changing sex roles on the family in later life', paper presented at Ford Foundation Conference on Changing Sex Roles in the Family, Merrill-Palmer Institute, Detroit, 1976
7 P Cotterill, *Friendly Relations? Mothers and their daughters-in-law*, Taylor Francis, London, 1994, p. 115
8 Cotterill, *op.cit.*, p. 69
9 P Cotterill, *op.cit.*, pp. 71–76
10 Bronwyn Donaghy, 'The big bad wolf behind granny', *Parents*, Sydney, February/March 1994
11 Alma Bond, *op.cit.*, p. 47
12 Fischer, *ibid.*
13 Eleanor Bailey, 'Divided families destroyed by hate', *Marie Claire*, March 1995

Chapter 11

1 Angela Lambert, 'Slaves to tiny tyrants', *Independent*, 16 November 1992
2 Barbara Brotman, 'Against the odds', *Parenting*, February 1995
3 K Strom, D Robert and Shirley Strom, *Becoming a Better Grandparent: Viewpoints on strengthening the family*, Sage, Newbury Park, California, 1991
4 Janet Robson, 'Is your little angel a computer killer?', *Independent*, 17 April 1995
5 Anna Quindlen, *The New York Times*, 21 June 1994, p. 7
6 Nicky Leap and Billie Hunter, *The Midwife's Tale*, Scarlet Press, London, 1993, p. 115
7 Interview with Jenny Kitzinger
8 Interview with Jenny Kitzinger
9 Alma H Bond, *op.cit.*, pp. 164–5
10 Sara Paretsky, *Blood Shot*, Dell, New York, 1988, p. 150
11 M Seligman, *Learned Optimism*, Knopf, New York, 1991
12 Bond, *op.cit.*, p. 55

Chapter 12

1 *I love my Granny and Grandpa too!*, op.cit.
2 Quoted in *Independent on Sunday*, 3 October 1993
4 William Blake, 'Auguries of Innocence' in *The Oxford Book of English Mystical Verse*, Clarendon Press, Oxford, 1949